Praise for *Intuition for Beginners*

Intuition for Beginners is a stimulating step-by-step guide to gaining a clearer and deeper understanding of tuning in to the world of intuition. The author of this wonderful book, Diane Brandon, takes the reader through a complex subject in a user-friendly style that only a true master of intuition could do!

—Bernie Ashman, astrologer, author of *SignMates* and *Sun Signs & Past Lives*

If you have ever had a question about intuition, this book will answer it. Diane Brandon demystifies intuition and teaches skills that are accessible to everyone. The meditations and exercises are easy to follow, and her clear and concise style will empower everyone to develop and use their natural intuition.

—Sherrie Dillard, psychic-medium and author of *Discover Your Psychic Type* and *Love and Intuition,* www.sherriedillard.com

Refreshingly, Diane is not promising that you will win the lottery or earn eternal love. What she does offer is a sober, clear, practical guide to understand, strengthen, and put to use your intuition. Packed with insight, exercises, and guided meditations, this book is for you if you are more interested in the genuine benefits intuition can bring to your life than in the party favors it may earn you.

—Valentine Leonard, PhD, spiritual counselor and creativity coach, author of *Bergson-Deleuze Encounters*

Intuition
for Beginners

NEW VISIONS BOOKS & GIFTS
2594 Eastern Blvd., York, PA 17402-2915
(717) 843-8067 or (800) 843-8067
Visit our website at www.newvisionsbooks.com
"For Peace of Mind, Body & Soul"

About the Author

Diane Brandon has been working professionally with her intuition as an Integrative Intuitive Counselor since 1992, and she has been teaching others how to access intuitive information on demand since 1996. She also teaches classes and seminars on dreams, personal empowerment, creativity, and listening skills, in addition to wellness classes, and offers corporate consulting.

She's the author of *Invisible Blueprints* and is a contributing author to *The Long Way Around* and *Speaking Out*. Her private work with clients focuses on facilitating personal development and life fulfillment, and she brings dream work, guided meditation, regression, Natural Process healing, and other modalities into her work. She has produced three meditation CDs and hosts a radio show, *Naturally Vibrant Living*. Born and raised in New Orleans, she has an A.B. from Duke University and did master's work at the University of North Carolina, in addition to French studies in Geneva, Switzerland. She's also a professional actor, singer, and voice-over artist.

Intuition

For Beginners

Easy Ways to Awaken Your Natural Abilities

DIANE BRANDON

Llewellyn Publications
Woodbury, Minnesota

FIRST EDITION
Fifth Printing, 2018

Cover art: Formal garden: iStockphoto.com/© Prill Mediendesign & Fotografie
Cover design by Lisa Novak
Edited by Andrea Neff

Llewellyn Publications is a registered trademark of Llewellyn Worldwide Ltd.

Library of Congress Cataloging-in-Publication Data
Brandon, Diane, 1948-
  Intuition for beginners : easy ways to awaken your natural abilities / by Diane Brandon. — First Edition.
      pages cm.
  Includes bibliographical references and index.
  ISBN 978-0-7387-3335-7
1. Psychic ability. 2. Psychic ability—Problems, exercises, etc. 3. Intuition. I. Title.
  BF1031.B734 2013
  153.4'4—dc23
                                    2012046581

Llewellyn Publications
A Division of Llewellyn Worldwide Ltd.
2143 Wooddale Drive
Woodbury, MN 55125-2989
www.llewellyn.com

Printed in the United States of America

There are things so deep and complex that only intuition can reach it in our stage of development as human beings.

—JOHN ASTIN

Acknowledgments

This book represents the culmination of many years of teaching and research, and many people have been part of that process.

I'd like to thank all my clients and students over the years. They have, by and large, been so pleasant to work with and have given me many wonderful insights and warmth, while enlarging my own knowledge and awareness of the ins and outs of intuition. I owe them a huge debt for their willingness to work with me and for all that I have gained from our work.

Close friends have also been supportive of my process and have my whole-hearted gratitude as well. I'd like to especially thank two good friends, Kathlyn Bushnell and Theresa Waltermeyer, who have walked the path of writing this book along with me by listening to my concerns and making suggestions.

I would like to thank everyone at Llewellyn for their belief in this book and assistance in its preparation, including Angela Wix, Andrea Neff, and Andy Belmas.

My hope is that all the effort put into the creation of this book may be fruitful for those who read it.

contents

introduction

Intuition can be a wonderful addition to your life. It is truly a many-splendored thing that will grace your life in a variety of ways because it can provide so many different benefits. If you're spiritually oriented, you can derive even more benefits from it, as it can help you tap into source (God, the Divine, the universe, the seat of all knowledge, etc.) and strengthen your spiritual connection.

Even though using your intuition can be hugely advantageous, it may seem out of reach at times for some people. The truth is that many people would like to use their intuition more to enrich their lives, but they just don't know how to go about doing so. This book will help you recognize your intuition, learn about its ins and outs, and develop and apply it to situations in your life.

My Story

I'm a firm believer in intuition and its many gifts. I've been working professionally with my intuition since 1992 as an Integrative Intuitive Counselor ("integrative" because I bring additional modalities into my work with clients). I have had many repeat clients and have been fortunate enough to consistently receive positive feedback on my abilities.

Even though working with my intuition has gone very well for me, the truth is that my intuitive ability came completely out of left field. I had always been fascinated by intuition and been deeply spiritual, but I certainly had never seen myself as intuitive. In fact, being intuitive or working with intuition was the furthest thing from my mind. Boy, was I surprised when I started working with mine! It opened a whole new world for me, which was even more surprising since it was so unexpected. Initially, after beginning to work with my intuition, I struggled, since intuition had previously seemed so foreign to me and I wasn't at all sure of what I was doing. However, I kept consistently receiving positive feedback from clients. So even though I had never seen myself as intuitive, I apparently was, which dumbfounded me.

Because my intuition had never been part of my self-definition or self-image, and because I've always had a need to *understand* things, I felt driven to figure out what intuition was and learn more about its uses and benefits. Through working with my own intuition, teaching it to others, observing my students, and conducting my own research, I started on a quest to understand the inner workings of intuition the best I could.

I now feel that I have a much firmer grasp of intuition than I originally did. I've been teaching intuitive techniques to others in workshops, seminars, and classes since 1996, and I love seeing others light up as they experience tapping into their intuition at will, often consciously for the first time. My growing understanding of intuition as a faculty has enabled me to become a better teacher. To my delight, I've seen student after student access their intuition and begin to gain confidence in their innate abilities.

Benefits of Intuition

Receiving intuitive information can be very enjoyable, but the benefits don't end there. There are many other benefits to using our intuition, both in our personal and work lives, other than just gaining information, and there may be some you haven't considered. The ones I've identified include the following:

- Intuition helps us make decisions.
- Intuition helps us solve problems.
- Intuition gives us more resources for information.
- Intuition helps us find and strengthen our inner voice and inner knowing.
- Intuition can give us more self-confidence and have empowering effects.
- Intuition can give us better insight into others.
- Intuition can help us have better relationships.

- Intuition can help us be present in the moment.
- Intuition can lead to greater objectivity and clearer perception.
- Intuition can lead us to be less reactive.

Let's look at each benefit in turn.

Intuition Helps Us Make Decisions

We all need to make decisions in our lives on a regular basis. This is just a part of life. In doing so, we look at all the details of the situation, and do research if necessary. Yet there are times when we still don't know which decision is the right one, even after we've done all that initial work, especially if there are several factors and options involved.

Using our intuition can be very helpful when it comes to making decisions. We may have a feeling and intuitively know which choice or direction is the right one. Intuition can even help us weigh different factors and know more about them, including their pros and cons—and even uncover factors we may not have considered. Our intuitive sense can tap us on the shoulder and point out problems we hadn't considered with some of the available options.

Intuition can also let us know when we're not ready to make a decision, even if we're champing at the bit to proceed and feel that we've already thought everything through. This can prevent future pain, because, if we make a decision prematurely and later find out that it was the wrong one, we will often find that additional problems have been created for us as a result.

Intuition can be a strong ally in helping us make the best decisions possible and at the optimum times.

Intuition Helps Us Solve Problems

It would be wonderful if we could always sail through life with no problems. This, of course, is not the nature of life. We will always have ups and downs and encounter problems that need to be sorted out, not just in our personal lives but at work as well.

Intuition can actually help us solve problems. It can point out hidden factors we may not have noticed or considered. There are times when we work at something and work at something, trying to figure out where the roadblock is—and find ourselves feeling continually stymied. However, our intuition will often show us exactly where the roadblock is and what we need to do about it.

Let's say you have a child who has started acting up in school. You might talk to the teacher about the problem. You might also talk to the school counselor and the principal—and a therapist and your minister or spiritual guide—all the while getting conflicting information and recommendations. This can be very confusing and frustrating.

You might even try some of the recommendations given to you, feeling uncertain about whether they're the right ones or whether they will work—but your intuition, if you know how to work with it, can let you know what the best thing to do would be and which approach would be best. With a honed intuitive sense, you can even try different approaches and know whether they feel right or not and which one will yield the best result.

Never underestimate the ability of your intuition to help you solve those troublesome problems in your life.

Intuition Gives Us More Resources for Information

Intuition can actually allow us to gain more information, because it increases our resources for information. We can know things through using our five senses and left-brain skills, of course, and intuition augments these. Our intuition can actually give us information that the rest of our mind can't, which is why we have the potential for this wonderful faculty.

Intuition is a wonderful resource to have, and you will probably find yourself increasingly glad you have it as you develop more of yours.

Intuition Helps Us Find and Strengthen Our Inner Voice and Inner Knowing

We all have an inner voice and an inner knowing, and being able to tap into this can be a wonderful and empowering thing. Tapping into our inner voice can help us find our own inner authority. Unfortunately, many people find it difficult to identify and then access their inner knowing, much less their inner authority. They may find themselves listening to everyone else but themselves. They may continually be looking for approval or value judgments from authorities and experts outside of themselves.

While we may still need to look for information outside of ourselves, we have the ability to develop our inner knowing and inner authority, leading us to know what feels right to us. Your inner voice can help you sort through a vast amount of external information and know what feels right to you. Your inner voice can serve as a strong guide, or inner rudder, in your life.

It is through tapping into our intuition that we find our inner voice, and it is through developing and strengthening our intuition that we also strengthen our inner knowing.

Your inner voice and inner knowing can lead you to be the master of your fate—and intuition will lead you to both of them.

Intuition Can Give Us More Self-Confidence and Have Empowering Effects

Intuition can also lead directly to greater self-confidence and self-empowerment. What is at the root of most self-doubt? Aside from an inability to accept who you are, it's an inability to tap into your inner voice and inner knowing. As we just examined, developing your intuition will lead you to strengthen your inner voice and inner knowing, leading to the development of your inner authority. As you find yourself more firmly planted in those, you will also find your self-doubt decreasing. You will find yourself becoming your own authority in your life.

Don't forget that, as you develop your inner voice and inner knowing, one thing that also gradually happens is that you find your yardstick for authority shifting from outside of you (what others feel is best) to inside of you (what you feel is best). This is how your inner authority comes to be. Developing your intuition can have incredibly self-empowering effects and give you greater self-confidence. It doesn't mean you will stop going outside of yourself for information or facts, but rather that you will know how to process that information and come to your own conclusions.

Intuition can give you some wonderful and empowering personal gifts.

Intuition Can Give Us Better Insight into Others

Some people are open books: what you see on the outside or surface of them is also what is on the inside. Not everyone is like this, though. Some people are quite complex, and we may have trouble understanding them or their actions as a result. We can develop problems in our relationships when we have trouble reading others and sensing where they're coming from, whether these are personal or work relationships.

This is another area in which intuition can be hugely beneficial: it can allow us to better read others—who they are on the inside and where they're coming from, and even what their needs are.

This is a specialty of mine in my work as an Integrative Intuitive Counselor, and I emphasize it in my teaching. Being able to have more insight into others can help us interact better with others and not misinterpret their actions. It can also allow us to innately sense whom to trust and whom not to. This can lead us to have better relationships, again both in our personal lives and at work.

Intuition Can Help Us Have Better Relationships

If you can have better insight into others and be less prone to misinterpret others' actions or where they're coming from, then you should also experience less conflict and fewer misunderstandings with others. So much of the conflict we encounter in our relationships stems from misunderstandings and hurt feelings. If you have an intuitive sense of where others are coming from—and then remember to use that application of intuition—you should have less conflict in your relationships. Of course it helps if both people or all parties involved are using their intuition as well.

We've all experienced conflict in our relationships, whether a perceived slight from a parent, an oversight in a romantic relationship, or negative feedback from a co-worker. Wouldn't it be wonderful to be less upset about such things and have fewer arguments or misunderstandings? The good news is that by using your intuition with others, you should find just that happening in your life.

Intuition Can Help Us Be Present in the Moment

"The world is too much with us," William Wordsworth wrote. And it's true. We live in a time of perpetual stimulation, with computers, television, street lights, and a 24/7 lifestyle. All this external stimulation tends to pull our attention outward, to what is going on around us, not to mention all the other demands of our lives, such as work, errands, and other responsibilities. As a result, we become continually attuned and "answerable" to what is outside of us.

Being centered, on the other hand, is a very different energy. When we're anchored in ourselves, we find ourselves calmer and less acted upon by all those external influences and demands. One thing that can lead us to become more centered is intuition.

When we're listening to our intuition, our attention is pulled inward. We withdraw our attention from external activities and suspend the moment. If you use the method presented in this book for accessing your intuition—what I call "tuning in"—you'll find yourself more centered as well as more focused in the moment.

This can lead you to be calmer—a wonderful thing, given how stressful our contemporary society is. If you find yourself stressed a great deal and experiencing a lot of mental spinning as you focus on all your to-dos and what-ifs, you'll likely find using your intuition to be a wonderful antidote.

Intuition Can Lead to Greater Objectivity and Clearer Perception

Many people don't realize that intuition can have this particular benefit, but it can indeed. As we just discussed, using our intuition can lead us to be more present in the moment and more centered. The more centered we are and the more present in the moment we are, the greater the likelihood that we'll also be more objective and clearer in our perceptions.

One thing that can affect and color our perceptions is personal "stuff," such as wants, fears, needs, mindsets, and beliefs. (Personal stuff can also color and contaminate intuitive information, which we'll discuss later on.) While our personal stuff is always there within us, affecting our perceptions, the truth is that the more stressed we are, the more likely it is that our personal stuff will be activated and will color our perceptions even more. As you learn to access your intuition through the method of tuning in and as you increasingly get into that clear place inside of you where your inner knowing resides, you'll find yourself less stressed and better able to be clear in your perceptions and more objective.

This heightened objectivity can spread out into every area of your life, as well as into events on the world stage. As you become more expert at using your intuition and become increasingly able to go to a place of clarity, you'll likely be able to see very objectively things going on in the world and what may be behind them. A spiritual orientation can also help you see the purpose for events on a higher level, from a higher perspective. This is a wonderful by-product of using your intuition, and it does depend on learning to tune in and using that method with your intuition.

Intuition Can Lead Us to Be Less Reactive

This benefit of intuition derives from the previous two. As we find ourselves more present in the moment and more objective, it just follows naturally that we'll find ourselves being less reactive. It's usually stress and our personal stuff, not to mention sensitivity and relationship problems, that lead us to be more reactive, as we find our buttons getting pushed more easily. However, the more centered and objective we are, the less "hot" our buttons will be and the less likely it will be for us to find ourselves negatively and spontaneously reacting to an irritating or painful stimulus.

Try This

Think of some experiences you've had over the years with your intuition, and make a list of them in a journal. As you review your experiences, can you identify any of the benefits discussed in this chapter manifesting as a result of what you experienced with your intuition? If you're already using your intuition on a regular basis, have you found yourself more centered, less reactive, less stressed, or positively affected when you use it?

What You Will Find in This Book

This book contains much of what I've learned about intuition and have taught to others over the years. It will help you learn more about how your intuition works and how to develop it and work with it. We'll start with some basics and cover a lot of different bases, because I feel that the more you understand the different aspects of intuition, the better equipped you'll be to develop and master your own.

You'll find many exercises in this book, both basic and advanced. You'll also find some other information that you may not have anticipated, such as things you can do with the intuitive information you receive. Simply receiving intuitive information is not the end of the story. There are other things we can, and often should, do with the information we've gotten. So you'll also learn about what to do *after* you've received that valuable intuitive information.

If you feel that you already know the ins and outs of intuition, you can always start with the exercises. You'll find meditative exercises in chapter 5, beginner ones in chapter 6, and advanced ones in chapter 9. Otherwise, allow yourself to explore some lesser-known facets of intuition in the early chapters and then move on to the exercises. If you're a beginner, please start with the exercises in chapter 5 and go through the ones in chapter 6 before trying the advanced ones in chapter 9. The meditative exercises in chapter 5 are the foundation for my method of tuning in. If you skip them, you will find it difficult to learn and master this method.

One thing that will aid you in developing your intuition as you move through this book is to keep a journal of your experiences. Make a note of your experiences with the exercises, as well as other realizations you have that are sparked by the material you find here. It will be immensely helpful for you to make journal entries and then review them from time to time. You should notice the progress you've made, in addition to having new insights.

This book is designed to take you on a journey to fully experience intuition, as you tour its different aspects and explore how it speaks to you. So prepare to go on that journey, a voyage that will see you more fully exploring and claiming for yourself this wonderful thing we call intuition.

one

Are You Intuitive?

Intuition is complex and, as a result, it can present itself in many different forms. It can also express itself very differently from one person to the next. Because of its complexity and seeming "shapeshifting," it can be hard to grasp what intuition really is. Some people might have experiences with their intuition and not even realize what it was. As a result, they may not see themselves as being intuitive.

It's also true that we might tend to feel that we're not intuitive if our intuition presents itself to us in a manner different from what we think intuition is. I had my own experience with this, because my intuition was certainly not acting the way I thought it would or should. It is very important to understand what intuition is in order to be able to develop and use your own. So let's work on that.

What Is Intuition?

One of the first steps toward understanding intuition is to define it in a way that makes sense and incorporates all its various aspects. I have asked students in my workshops and classes over the years what intuition is. They generally answer that it's a feeling or an inner voice—and that is true. However, the truth is that these are *forms* of intuition, but they don't define *what* intuition is. To get a true understanding of intuition, we need a working definition of it that includes all of the many ways and forms in which it can manifest.

Because intuition can present itself in many different ways—it can be a real trickster at times—we'll need to define it quite broadly. Here is the working definition I have devised after studying it for over fourteen years:

> **Intuition** is the accessing of information through means other than our customary logical mode—our intellect—or our five recognized senses. It's a way of knowing things without going through the intellect or the five tangible senses or how we normally experience and know things in life.

Allow yourself to read that over a few times. You'll see that it's a broad enough definition to include different aspects of intuition and the many faces it can have. Does this definition make sense to you and fit your own experiences with intuition?

Examples of Intuition

Now that you have a definition, let's look at some examples of intuition expressing itself to people in different ways:

- Pete walks into the classroom where he teaches and suddenly feels a wash of elation come over him that he feels in his body. That day, a student who had been a consistent troublemaker has a positive breakthrough.

- Bob is preparing for a presentation to a new client whom he has heard has a reputation for being really difficult. In spite of what he's heard, Bob senses that his presentation will go well and that he'll develop a good relationship with the new client.

- Anna is a novelist and has been struggling over one particular passage in her new book. After going to bed one night, she lies awake puzzling over the chapter and then falls asleep. In the morning when she wakes up, she realizes that she knows exactly how to write the chapter.

- Charles knows that he laid his notepad down in his apartment, but he can't find it. He looks all over for about twenty minutes, then gives up. He sits down at his computer and works for about an hour. When he finishes, he gets up and walks to exactly where his notepad is.

- Steve is a nurse in a busy medical practice where patients often experience long waits before seeing him and eventually the doctor. No matter how upset and cranky the patients are, Steve has an unfailing ability to get on their wavelengths, sense their moods, know how to approach them, and get them to smile.

- Amy can always sense what her daughter Ruth is going through, no matter how far apart they might be. One day when Ruth fell off a horse at camp, Amy knew exactly at that moment that something had happened to Ruth.

- Christine manages a large veterinary practice with three employees at a time working the front desk. Two of them used to be close friends, but have been squabbling with each other for months. Christine has been concerned about how the employees' animosity toward each other and the resulting tension might be affecting clients, but has been stymied in figuring out how to deal with the situation. One day after lunch, Christine has a sudden insight about how to deal with the situation. She speaks to the two employees, and the misunderstanding is resolved, with them getting along and peace reigning once again in the practice.

- George has been doing some groundbreaking research into subtle energy. He has a new concept of some aspects of subtle energy and has worked up a mathematical model of it. All the details add up mathematically. However, George senses that something is not accurate or is missing. He continues to analyze his model, continually missing what might be off. Although he is under pressure from others to release his concept and get it published, he hesitates. One day while jogging, he suddenly knows what the problem is. He revises his model with everything now in place.

- Rosalind has been planning to go to a late showing of a film she has wanted to see for some time. She has had to delay seeing it because the times it was being shown didn't fit her schedule. On this day, the late showing works best for her. At the last minute, however, she suddenly feels an urge to go to an earlier showing and rearranges her schedule. After she gets home, a violent storm breaks out that she would have been caught in had she gone to the later showing.

- David has been doing day trading for some years with modest success. He has a hunch about a company and places a trade. Within two months, the stock doubles.

- Pam is getting ready for bed. She turns out the light and then suddenly hears her father's voice say, "I love you." Her mother calls a few minutes later to tell her that her father passed away—at exactly the time Pam heard his voice.

- Sherry has been in an abusive relationship for several years, which has been so bad that friends and co-workers have been worried about her. One day while out grocery shopping, she sees a flyer for a new women's shelter that just opened that offers services to women in abusive relationships. Even though she's interested, Sherry feels that people in her socioeconomic position are not those who could be clients of such services. The next day she turns on the TV just as a segment starts on getting out of abusive relationships. She watches it with some interest and is surprised to learn that spousal abuse is not limited to people in any one specific socioeconomic group.

Sherry suddenly has an aha moment about her situation and realizes that she can get help and get out of the abusive relationship. Sherry feels encouraged and calls the center.

- Kyle has been single for several years but has wanted to be in a good relationship. He has always remembered someone he had been in love with in high school but who married someone else after he went off to college. He still thinks of her with regret. One night he dreams about her, and in his dream she is no longer married. A few days later in a conversation with his mother, he learns that his old flame has indeed recently divorced. He calls her and the two of them start seeing each other again.

As you can see from these examples, intuition can come to us in different ways and in a whole range of situations—and will usually grace our lives as a result.

Why Some People Recognize Intuition More Than Others

One of the biggest concerns I've heard students express over the years is whether they are indeed intuitive. Do you ever find yourself wondering if you are or not? Well, let me reassure you right off the bat that practically everyone has intuitive ability. You would be hard-pressed to find someone who doesn't have intuitive potential to some degree, unless there's some sort of physical brain or psychological abnormality.

Intuition seems to be something we all have as a potential, although it may be dormant or hidden in many of us. Even if it has been dormant or hidden in you, please know that you are bound to be intuitive and may just need to find and develop your intuition.

Have you ever known who was calling when the phone rang? Or have you ever felt like taking a different route to work or school on a whim, and then been glad later on that you did? Perhaps you might have had a good or bad feeling about a person on sight, and then had that instinct confirmed. Has that ever happened to you? Have you ever known what a friend or family member was going to say before he or she started talking? Or have you ever thought of a song and turned on the radio or changed stations and heard it playing?

Examples of everyday, mundane intuition abound, and I would be surprised if you had never had any experiences with your own intuition. Even people who might scoff at the idea of intuition have usually had some intuitive experiences of their own—although they might have discounted them—simply because most people have innate intuitive ability, whether they believe in it or not.

That said, for some people, intuition is just closer to the surface and more naturally accessible. I've noticed for years that there seems to be a correlation between a more natural intuitive ability and creativity, artistic ability, and spirituality, and that people with these characteristics spontaneously have more intuitive experiences. Research has shown that this may be due to different brain wave states that seem to be more the norm for people with these attributes. I have these attributes and know firsthand that this is true. So if you find yourself to be creative (including creative thinking), artistic, or spiritual, you may indeed find that uncovering your intuitive gifts is fairly easy to do. And even if you haven't uncovered them yet, you may find it an easier thing to do than other people without those attributes. That said, even people without these characteristics will generally have intuitive potential. It's simply a matter of being taught how to uncover and access it.

Being compassionate or empathetic also seems to indicate a more natural intuitive ability. Additionally, how we feel about someone else can help determine how easy or how difficult it is to get intuitive information about the person, and there's actually science behind this. A lot of research has been conducted on the heart, health, and emotions by the Institute of HeartMath in California, including the finding that the heart has its own awareness. This research has shown, among other things, how much our heart affects our health—and the health of others. Our heart waves extend out from our bodies and can affect others' brain waves when we touch. Our hearts can have either a positive or negative effect on others and ourselves. The factor that determines whether the effect will be positive or negative is the type of emotions we feel. Positive feelings will bring about a positive effect, and negative emotions will bring about a negative effect. This research explains why, when we feel positive toward someone, it may be easier to get on the person's wavelength and sense things intuitively about him or her. It is easier to get intuitive information about someone else if we open our heart and feel love or appreciation for the person.

Compassion and empathy help to grease the wheels, so to speak, in opening to someone else and attempting to access intuitive information about him or her. Of course, it never hurts to be a compassionate, empathetic person to begin with—unless we have difficulty putting up a boundary when necessary and find ourselves too open too often, which we'll discuss in more detail later on.

Speaking of boundaries, it would appear that people with thin boundaries also tend to be more naturally intuitive. The concept of boundaries, if you're not familiar with it, has generally derived from psychology. As it turns out, there are different boundaries, the first being between people—in other words, between other people and you. Another boundary is that between this three-dimensional reality and other, more spiritual levels or planes of existence. If that boundary for you is somewhat thin—that is, if you're naturally or inherently spiritual—then it's likely that you'll take to intuition like a duck to water.

We also have a boundary between our conscious awareness and our subconscious/unconscious. It seems almost impossible to get a glimpse into our unconscious mind, which is why it's termed the unconscious. However, if you've meditated for a length of time, you know that as you meditate more often, you do indeed get glimpses into those deeper levels of yourself and more information on what lies in your unconscious. I'm a huge proponent of meditation and actually use guided meditation with clients for several different purposes: to meet guides (our spiritual guides), to begin to get answers from within, and even to work on personal issues and remove blocks to potential. (Please note that whenever I refer to "guides," I mean spiritual guides.) Meditation is also intrinsic to the method I use and teach for accessing intuitive information, called tuning in, which we'll explore in chapter 4.

The thinner the boundary is between our conscious and unconscious minds, the likelier it is that we'll be more naturally intuitive. Certain customary states of mind with more alpha brain waves (which are also linked to creativity, as it turns out) tend to be more conducive to a thinner boundary between what we're consciously aware of and what lies in our unconscious. Alpha brain waves are a little slower than our normal waking brain waves, called beta brain waves. We tend to spend most of our time awake in beta, when we're focusing on something or even stressing.

Belleruth Naparstek, in her excellent book *Your Sixth Sense*, writes that she feels that people who have "bilateral dominance" (being whole-brain rather than predominantly right- or left-brain) or who are dyslexic, musical, artistic, emotionally sensitive, imaginative, spontaneous, and/or inherently spiritual, have natural intuitive ability. These are some of the attributes already cited. Dissociation (a psychological condition in which a part of one's consciousness is not "present" but is split off and which often derives from severe trauma or abuse) has also been said to predispose those with it to being more naturally intuitive.

People who have had a near-death experience often find their intuitive abilities heightened or emerging as a result of their experience. Many of them almost seem to have been "rewired" by their experience. Near-death experiences can have many significant after-effects on those who have them, not the least of which is heightened intuition.

Interestingly, I have heard from several massage therapists over the years who saw their intuition developing naturally after they started working in this field. I suspect that while doing this type of work, practitioners shift their focus from a task-driven awareness to an awareness of what their hands are feeling and picking up on, representing a shift in consciousness to one that is more conducive to intuition.

I also feel that people who tend to be more introspective and inner-directed are more likely to have natural intuitive ability.

Children tend to be innately intuitive. Those who have "invisible friends" may be seeing presences (or spirits) rather than imagining that they have nonexistent playmates. Children's brain waves differ from those of teenagers and adults. They have more alpha and delta brain waves, which research shows are more conducive to intuition. Children also tend to be more creative as well as more openly loving. For these reasons, children's intuitive ability is inherently and naturally stronger or closer to the surface. However, if family members and others don't encourage this ability, the intuitive abilities may weaken or disappear as the children get older. I have repeatedly encountered people who recalled being intuitive when they were little but who felt that they had lost the ability. If this feels familiar, let me reassure you that you haven't lost the ability. It's still there and you can reclaim it.

Research has been conducted in China on children's psychic abilities as far back as 1980 and continuing into the present. This research, which I've found cited on several websites (see the bibliography), indicates that children are more likely to exhibit *psi* (another term for psychic ability) than adults and that the ability appears to decline after the age of fourteen. These studies use the terms *psi* and *psychic*, but I feel that there is little or no difference between intuition and psychic phenomena, although the latter term can also include phenomena such as mind over matter (or psychokinesis).

I also suspect that academic training leads children to rely increasingly on their left-brain intelligence and tamp down intuitive input and right-brain skills. This doesn't mean, however, that we can't be intuitive if we had a strong academic background. I have a rigorous academic background, although I also pursued creative activities such as singing and acting—and I found tapping into my intuition to be fairly easy (even if I didn't know what I was doing initially). So if you have a strong academic background, you should still find that you can learn to tap into and develop your intuition. The two are definitely not mutually exclusive.

That said, our academic training can hinder our intuitive expression if we're not balancing it with right-brain activities. In addition, I would say that since the Age of Reason in the 17th century, with its emphasis on rationalism, and with the ascendancy of science, we've seen a growing cultural attitude that only the rational/empirical and that which stems from our five senses can be trusted. As a result, there are cultural attitudes that don't encourage the use of intuition. However, that needn't be a block to developing our intuitive abilities.

So, are you intuitive, even if you don't recognize any of the markers I've discussed as describing you?

I would wager that you are. Most people can learn how to find and develop their intuition. No matter whether you have any of the markers for more naturally expressed intuition, you should be able to access your intuition and learn to develop it. It's just a matter of being taught how.

I've learned through my own intuitive work and through teaching intuition since 1996 that you can learn to tap into your intuition by varying your state of consciousness. I will be teaching you exactly how to do that in this book. However, I've also learned that it's not just a matter of learning how to enter into those states of mind that are conducive to intuition; it's also a matter of understanding what intuition is and isn't, so you can recognize it and then cultivate it. Until you understand intuition better, you might not be able to recognize it, much less be able to take advantage of the insights and gifts it can provide.

So the next thing we're going to do is learn some of the basics about intuition.

two

Your Basic 411 on Intuition

Now that you have a broad definition of intuition, the next important step in using your intuitive ability is learning how it works for *you* and how it presents itself to *you*. Just because you have a friend who has an inner voice that speaks to her doesn't mean that you're not intuitive if you're not experiencing the same thing. This is a biggie, because we can look right past our own intuition if it's not behaving in the way we think it will. I struggled initially in working with my intuition because I wasn't experiencing what I thought intuitive people did. For example, I expected that information would strike me out of the blue if I was intuitive, but my intuition was definitely not direct or striking. Mine preferred to be really subtle.

Just because your friend's intuition comes in the form of an inner voice doesn't mean that yours will—or should. Your intuition may express itself by more of a sense—an abstract sense—about things, for example, or you may tend to get visual information, in the form of images. Allow yourself to realize that you have your own unique expression of intuition, and don't let anyone tell you how your intuition *should* work! It's a misconception that it works the same way for everyone. Allow yourself to explore your intuition with an open mind about how it will appear to you and speak to you.

The intuition you want to develop is *your* intuition, not someone else's. In order to use your intuition, you have to first recognize it—how it expresses itself to *you* and in which forms—and then cultivate it. The better you understand intuition and recognize your own, the better equipped you'll be to use it and reap its benefits.

Forms of Intuition

Intuition can come to us in a variety of ways and situations. Because there are so many different forms of intuition, you'll find many different expressions of intuition, not just from one person to the next, but also even from one intuitive event to another. Let's look at what these various forms are:

- **Hunches:** I often think of businesspeople having hunches, but anyone can have a hunch about something. For lack of a better way of putting it, you just get an inner nudge about something.

- **Gut feelings:** A gut feeling comes through your gut or stomach feeling different. You may have a queasy feeling when contemplating an upcoming meeting, for example. Gut feelings are very common, although our bodies can pick up on information in places other than our gut. You'll find more information on this later in this chapter under "Bodily Awareness."

- **Sudden insights, realizations, and ahas:** This form occurs when something comes to you in a sudden realization, what some call a "light bulb moment." All of a sudden, something makes perfect sense to you, or an idea or realization comes to you.

- **Illuminating dreams:** A dream may be precognitive and give you information about a future event, or a dream may be clairvoyant and give you information about a family member at a distance. Intuition doesn't limit itself to speaking to us only while we're awake. It can also be active while we're sleeping, and it can creep into our dreams, whether subtly or blatantly.

- **The visual or images in the mind's eye (also called clairvoyance, French for "clear seeing"):** When our intuition comes in a visual form, we may see a picture or even a vision. This can come through our eyes, and we actually see something, or it can be figurative, and a picture forms in our minds (just think about picturing someone else in your mind). Whether seen literally through the eyes or in the form of an imagined image in the mind, intuitive information that comes in a visual form is far from uncommon.

- **Instincts:** Some people may not consider instincts to be intuition, but instincts can be either quite close to or an expression of intuition. If you encounter an unknown animal, for example, your instincts may lead you to know whether to run from it or not.

- **Nagging feelings that just won't go away:** Have you ever gotten intuitive information and talked yourself out of listening to it? There may be when your intuitive feelings just won't go away. For example, you may be house-hunting and you find a house that seems to be perfect for you, but you keep having a feeling of avoidance about following through on buying it. You may try to talk yourself out of the avoidance, but the nagging feeling just won't go away. That may be your intuition giving you a message.

- **Impressions:** Intuitive information that comes in the form of an impression is vague and can be challenging to work with. The information is there and you sense that it is and can sense some of it, but it can be so vague or diffuse that you're not really sure what it is. A lot of the information I receive comes in the form of an impression, so I know how difficult impressions can be to work with. You sense the information there, but can't quite get it to form more definitively so that you can be sure of what it is. Over time, however, impressions can become easier to handle as you practice working with them.

- **Hearing—an auditory sense (also called clairaudience, French for "clear hearing"), which could be of a voice or sound, including the inner voice:** This form of hearing will be pretty obvious, although, as with visual forms, it can be literal or figurative. You may actually hear a voice or a sound through your ears, or you may hear a sound in your mind, as if you were imagining a sound. Our senses, when it comes to intuition, can be both inner and outer. We also talk about listening to our "inner voice," so we will include the inner voice here as a hearing form of intuition. It's necessary, however, to distinguish between our true inner intuitive voice and old tapes that come from negative things we were consistently told during our formative years.

- **Smell (sometimes referred to as clairgustance, although this term doesn't exist in French):** Your intuition can also come to you in the form of smell. For example, if you're getting information on a negative subject, you may suddenly smell an unpleasant odor. Metaphorically the subject may "stink." Smell is also one of the common ways in which passed-on loved ones will try to communicate with friends or family left behind. Many people have reported smelling the familiar perfume or cologne of a loved one who has transitioned. (This often happens because the deceased person wants to let his or her loved one know that he or she is okay and can't find another way to get through. I know people who don't believe in after-death communication who have experienced this.) This type of after-life communication is not limited to humans. Animals may also attempt to let us know they're okay after they've passed by transmitting their body's smell to their owner. I have experienced this myself firsthand.

- **Touch (also known as psychometry and sometimes referred to as clairsentience, French for "clear feeling," although the French term also includes feeling and awareness in addition to touch):** Intuition can come in the form of touch, usually through a person touching an object or even through touching someone else. This form of intuition is referred to as psychometry. With objects, information from the object's history may be conveyed by touching it. An object or another person can also be a triggering device for an intuitive person to receive information from touching it or the person. Some intuitives and psychics specialize in this form of intuition and may work with police departments to help solve crimes, such as murders or missing-person cases. They will hold an object—a sweater or a scarf, for example—belonging to the victim or missing person and receive intuitive impressions and information.

  Some people also receive information about other people through touching the person, such as touching another person's arm, hand, or back. I knew a woman years ago who needed to hold a person's hand in order to read him or her.

  I usually include an exercise in psychometry (using objects) in my intuition workshops and classes, as participants may have an unexpected gift with this form, and you'll find an exercise on this in chapter 6. I also feel that people who work with their hands, such as massage therapists, sculptors, and potters, may develop this form and find information coming to them via their hands while they're working.

• **Sensitivity to energy, whether it's that of a person, an animal, nature, etc.:** Another lesser-known form of intuition is sensitivity to energy. We can actually receive intuitive information through our exposure to energy—whether it's a person's energy, a place's energy, an animal's energy, or the energy of a situation—by intuitively sensing the energy. I experience this form quite often.

Additionally, some people may be able to see other people's energy. People who can read auras can usually see them, whether it's the aura of a person, an animal, or even a plant. I sense others' energy rather than seeing it, and you may find that you can sense energy in ways other than seeing it.

Everything is composed of energy, and we can be intuitive enough to sense it. As you develop your intuition, you may find your sensitivity increasing (as your boundaries get thinner) and you may find yourself sensing energy in ways you hadn't before.

Energy contains information, and indeed, information itself is energy. So a sensitivity to energy will usually convey information that can be used or will be helpful in some way.

• **Kinesthetic feelings:** Intuitive information can come to you in the form of a feeling other than touch. You may be able to feel a situation, for example.

Let's say you walk into a room in which three people are speaking to each other. You note that your body feels different—you may suddenly feel stiff or heavier. A kinesthetic feeling is one you feel in your body that's usually other than touch and may even be non-specific.

- **Telepathy:** Telepathy is a fairly well-known form of intuition. It's mind-to-mind communication, in which two people are communicating although they may not have a conscious awareness that it's happening. On occasion I have found myself thinking about a client I haven't spoken to in a while, and usually I hear from him or her a few days later. In those instances, I was apparently unconsciously picking up on their thinking of me.

  Telepathy can occur while we're awake and also while we're asleep. (You'll learn more about this in the appendix, when we look at how to work with dreams.)

  Telepathy can be very common between two people who are close to each other. When we get close to someone else, we become more attuned to him or her and will be on the person's wavelength. Our inner radar is "tuned" to the other person, and we may sense what he or she is experiencing. Our energy fields can actually become entwined when we're close to someone. With this type of closeness, we can sense when something may be wrong with him or her at a distance and we will often communicate with each other on a deep level, whether or not we have a conscious awareness of the communication.

Telepathy isn't restricted to communication with other people. We can experience it with animals as well, which is what animal communicators specialize in.

- **Seeing or sensing presences:** Another form of intuition is that of seeing or sensing presences. These presences can include passed-on people or animals ("ghosts" or spirits), guides, or other beings.

  Some people specialize in this form and may have always had the ability to see or sense presences.

- **Bodily awareness, such as goose bumps, chills, etc. (also called "embodied cognition"):** Your body can register and communicate information. This form of intuition is also called embodied cognition and includes such signals as goose bumps, a chill, etc., that let you know whether something feels right or not. We can include gut feelings in this category as well. Research in the past few years has shown a scientific basis for them and for an awareness in the gut.

  Your heart also has awareness, including precognitive awareness. We know this now thanks to research conducted by the Institute of HeartMath, which I discussed previously.

  The only problem with working with this form of intuition is that it can be a challenge to figure out what your body has registered. We will discuss a way to work with this later on.

- **Combinations of forms:** We can have instances in which we receive information that comes in more than one form. For example, we may receive some information about a situation and then get a chill of foreboding in our body, or we may receive an image of something while also hearing a voice. Intuition is all about information and gaining information, so we're actually fortunate if that information can come to us in more than one way or form.

  Over time, you may find that you experience certain forms of intuition more than others. However, you'll want to stay open to experiencing different forms. *Remember to allow yourself to be open to receiving intuitive information in different ways and different forms.*

- **Unrecognized perceptual modes:** Even though we've discussed many different ways in which intuition can present itself to us, I feel that there are still other forms that we haven't identified yet, which I'll call unrecognized perceptual modes. I know from reading clients' essences over the years that there is great individuality insofar as essence is concerned and how people's energy may work. (Essence refers to who a person uniquely is on the inside in the present lifetime, underneath anything layered on top that's not who he or she truly is—such as beliefs, mindsets, fear, desires, etc. Your essence is the purest you on the deepest level in the present lifetime and is usually a powerful indicator of your path and purpose in life.) As I've read clients' essences over the years, I've gotten things I had never even thought of, such as one person's ability to hear nature.

I'm sure science will catch up one day and identify those modes. In the meantime, just know that they're out there and you may find yourself experiencing them.

As you can see, intuition can appear to us in many different forms. If you've had experiences with your intuition, this may not come as a surprise to you. Whether or not this surprises you, I feel that it speaks to the richness of intuitive experiences. The fact that there are myriad forms of intuition only underscores how complex intuition can be.

Have we identified all the forms in which intuition can manifest? I feel that we'll find even more in the future. This is why we can feel ill-equipped at times to define intuition and why one person's sense of it can differ so greatly from another person's. Because of this, it's important to be open to all the ways in which intuition may speak to you.

Some people may even disagree about what intuition is like because of how differently it can express itself from one time to another and from one person to another. Each person may see or experience intuition solely from his or her point of view or personal experience with it, and may thus see only one facet of it and be unable to grasp the entire phenomenon. Some people have even argued about what intuition is because their individual experiences of it were so different. And yet, even though different people may have completely divergent experiences of intuition, it's still all intuition presenting itself with different faces.

The types of intuitive information received can also vary from person to person. Different people may primarily get certain types of information that differ from what others receive. For example, some people may primarily get information about events that will happen in the future, while others may get only information about negative impending events or be best at finding lost objects. Still others may be more attuned to what others are thinking or feeling. Although I get information about a range of topics, my intuitive counseling work with individuals tends to focus on the following things: what people are like on the inside (their essence); where they are in their process of unfolding; the higher meaning of what they are dealing with; how they may best handle the situations they're presented with or relationships they're in; their life path and purpose; diverse insights that could be useful to them; and how they can facilitate their process of unfolding and evolving for life improvement, greater personal fulfillment, and more internal resources.

As far as the *type* of information that intuition can give us is concerned, there generally is no limit, and each person may be more attuned to certain types of information and less so to others.

What is the lesson in all this? *Never tell yourself—or let anyone else tell you—that you have to experience intuition in a certain way or only get certain types of information. Allow yourself to become acquainted with YOUR intuition in all its ways of speaking to you.*

Try This

Look at the list of your experiences with intuition over the years that you made in the introduction to this book. Given how we have defined intuition, are there any more experiences you've had that you could consider intuitive? Which forms did your intuition come in? Have you ever had your intuition express itself to you in a combination of forms? Make a note in your journal about what you've experienced.

Attributes of and Ways in Which Intuition Appears

The multifaceted nature of intuition extends to more than the forms in which it can appear. Intuition can also vary in its feel, its attributes, and its characteristics. It can be a real shapeshifter! This aspect of intuition really took me by surprise. When I first started working with my intuition, I kept expecting it to appear in the way that I had heard it did—out of the blue and suddenly. I had heard that it would just hit you and be striking and undeniable. You would immediately know what it meant, with no uncertainty. Well, unfortunately that didn't happen for me. My intuition didn't speak to me that way, and my reaction was to feel that either I was not intuitive or that my intuitive information was not accurate.

I finally came to learn that I am indeed intuitive. I just needed to change my ideas about how intuition works.

If you've been assuming that intuition works the same way for everyone or that you're not very intuitive because you're not like your friend who has strong intuition, please allow yourself to realize how very chameleon-like intuition can be. Just as it will come in many different forms, so too will intuition have many different "feels" to it. I personally think that that's one of the beauties of intuition.

Because intuition can be so multifaceted, it will be helpful for you to know some of the ways in which it can present itself, so you will be better equipped to recognize it when it presents itself to you. This should help you claim more of your ability and develop your intuition to a greater extent.

Let's look some of the varied attributes of intuition.

Intuition Speaks to Us Whether We're Awake or Asleep

Intuition isn't limited to speaking to us just while we're awake. It can be present at any time, irrespective of our schedule or whether we're sleeping. We'll look at how intuition presents itself to us in dreams in the appendix. For now, just know that it can be present round the clock. Just like New York City, intuition doesn't sleep!

We Don't Always Know That We Know

This heading may sound a little strange, but intuitive information can come to us without our conscious awareness that it has come in or is even there—at least until it surfaces into the light of our conscious awareness. In other words, we can receive intuitive information without knowing that it has come in. To complicate matters, intuitive information doesn't always come from outside of us. Sometimes it comes from within us, from the inner workings of our consciousness and mind.

Have you ever had something suddenly pop into your mind that you hadn't known that you knew? This can really be surprising when it happens, and you might have thought, "Where did that come from?" Similarly, you may not always be aware of intuitive information coming to you or when it comes. Even though this sounds a bit odd, it's really not uncommon.

We can also have intuitive information come to us without our knowing what it's about. Have you ever thought about someone you hadn't seen or spoken to in years and then you heard from the person? I think most of us have experienced this, and I just experienced it—again—while writing this section. I found myself thinking of someone who had been a somewhat regular customer in a performing arts store I owned over twenty years earlier. I hadn't thought of her in more years than I could remember. Then two days after she crossed my mind, she connected with me on Facebook.

If you've ever found yourself knowing something and wondering how you came to know it, this is probably intuition. To put it simply, sometimes we'll be aware of receiving an intuitive insight and other times we won't, because it will have come in on the unconscious level. This makes intuition even more complex, doesn't it?

Intuition Is Not Always in the Mind

Intuitive information doesn't always present itself in the mind alone. It can also come in the body. We discussed this somewhat in the previous section on the forms of intuition, as you'll recall, and you'll remember the examples of gut feelings or goose bumps.

Bodily intuitive information can include more than gut feelings or goose bumps, though.

I had one strongly memorable experience with picking up on something intuitively through my body. It happened with Hurricane Katrina in 2005.

The week before Katrina hit, I started to not feel well. At first I thought I was just fighting a bug. The following day, Wednesday, the sick feeling was still there, and each day that week it seemed to grow worse.

That Friday was the first day that weather forecasters mentioned that a hurricane named Katrina was off the coast of Florida. When I heard that, I felt a glimmer of something deep inside, a slight movement or flash, although I didn't quite know what it was.

I continuously monitored the weather reports of Katrina, as I do with many hurricanes.

That weekend, I felt increasingly sick, while my conscious mind kept wondering what this was all about. Even on Monday after Katrina had made landfall and newscasters declared New Orleans to be safe, I was still sick to my stomach.

The next morning, Tuesday, when I heard that the levees had broken in New Orleans and the city was starting to flood, I knew why I had been so sick to my stomach.

You see, I was born and raised in New Orleans. I lived there for over eighteen years until I went off to college. I lived there again between college and grad school and went down once or twice a year to visit my parents and see friends.

If there ever was an experience that taught me that gut feelings could be real or express a precognitive awareness of an event, this was it. This experience also taught me that our energy field can be entwined not just with those of people we're close to, but also with places we're close to or have lived in. They're a part of us on some level, and when something happens to them, we register it on a deep level inside, even imperceptibly at times, with just a gnawing at us in some indefinable way. For me it had been that sick feeling and a weeklong nausea.

Never discount your body's intuitive potential or its potential to give you information. Your body definitely perceives and registers information, even before the fact.

Intuition Is a Receiving of Information

Generally speaking, intuition is receptive, in that it's a *receiving* of information. You suddenly have an awareness come to you, an image presents itself to you, you receive an impression—these are examples of intuition being receptive. In other words, the information comes to you rather than you seeking it out, which would be an active mode. Compare that receiving of information to your left brain, which works in an active way by analyzing, comparing, dissecting, and so forth.

That said, some aspects of your intuition may seek out information. Consider the inner radar you have, which is continually sussing out the environment for relevant or helpful information. When it finds information for you, you still then need to receive it.

It's important to remember that intuition is receptive, because if we chase after information, we may push it away. You'll want to be in a receptive mode to receive intuitive information.

Intuition Can Be Subtle or Blatant

One important thing to remember about your intuition is that the information you receive can be subtle or blatant. Some people may not recognize that their intuition is speaking to them if the information is subtle. I know that I kept feeling that I couldn't be intuitive when I first started working with my intuition because I thought information would suddenly strike me in a direct way—and it wasn't striking me. Initially it drove me crazy at times. I thought that the information would be obvious or blatant and I would just know things. That, however, is not how my intuition usually works. A great deal, if not most, of the time my information is subtle, sometimes maddeningly so. Over time, however, I accepted that and gradually learned how to work with all types of information, even the subtle type.

With blatant information, you usually have no doubt about what it's about or that you've received it. An example of blatant intuition would be a sudden urge to do something. When the information is subtle, however, you might have to work at determining its meaning.

Impressions can often be subtle, as mentioned earlier, and much of the information I receive is quite subtle. I often have to work at determining what it is, what it refers to, and even what it means.

Please don't dismiss information that is subtle. Such information is not at all less reliable than blatant or obvious information. It simply has a different feel and quality to it—but it's valid intuitive information nonetheless.

No matter whether you tend to receive one type more than the other, allow yourself to be open to receiving both subtle and blatant intuitive information, and treat the subtle information with the same respect that you accord to the blatant information. In time, you'll learn how to work with both types of information.

Intuition Can Be Literal or Symbolic

Intuitive information can also be either literal or symbolic. Literal information is easier to work with, since we usually know right away what the information means. Symbolic information, on the other hand, like symbolic imagery in dreams, can be more difficult to work with, as we may struggle to tease out its meaning. This can make intuition less than user-friendly at times, until we learn, through practice, how to work with this aspect of intuition. Obviously, intuitive information is usually the most helpful when we know what it means.

To complicate matters, we can access information at times that may be difficult to discern in terms of whether it's literal or symbolic. Once again, we can learn to overcome this seeming obstacle with practice. I'll give suggestions on how to work with this later in the book. Learning to work with and refine our intuition is not always a straightforward process. Using intuition can be more of an art than a science at times, but we can indeed improve and make great strides. And, because of all the gifts intuition can give us, it's definitely worth the time and effort.

Factoid or Nonquantifiable

It's important to know that we can receive many kinds of intuitive information, including both information representing facts and that which is nonquantifiable. Many people expect that intuitive information will be restricted solely to quantifiable information, such as a name, a date, a statistic, or a number. Indeed, a great deal of research on ESP has focused on studying this type of information.

However, we can receive many different types of information, much of it nonquantifiable, such as the feel of a situation, what someone is feeling, and so forth. My Katrina experience involved nonquantifiable information—that sick feeling.

When I read a client's essence—what he or she is like on the deepest level inside—that information is nonquantifiable. If you receive information about the feel of a situation, the information will be nonquantifiable.

There is a tendency among some people to hold nonquantifiable information in lower regard than factoids. This should not be the case, however. All types of intuitive information are valuable and should be considered valid. What matters is how we handle the information and what we do with it, which we'll be looking at later on. For example, when conveying nonquantifiable information to others, we may need to take extra care to describe it in a clear and understandable manner.

If you've accessed intuitive information that's nonquantifiable, allow yourself to value it, as you've received it for a reason. You may need to do additional work to understand it, but it should be valuable nonetheless.

Intuition Can Have a Calm, Urgent, or Positive Feeling

It's important to realize that the intuitive information you receive can have a range of feels attached to it. While a lot of information can feel calm or neutral, lacking any emotional coloration, not all information will feel that way. If you get information giving you a valuable insight, it could feel positive. Conversely, you could also receive information about a negative future event—an accident, for example. Obviously, that information about the accident wouldn't necessarily have a good feeling attached to it. It would feel negative. Similarly, if you receive information that represents a warning about something, that information is also not likely to feel good.

While I would generally say that if you're centered while receiving information (using my procedure for tuning in, which we'll go over in chapter 4), you will tend to receive information that feels calm or neutral, the truth is that that will not always be the case. It's important to realize this and not expect all the information you get to feel just one way. Remember that being open will allow your intuition to bloom even more.

Intuition Is Clear and Uncolored by Personal Stuff

What we're going to cover here is extremely important, so please treat this section as if it were highlighted or redlined.

The only intuitive information you can trust or put any credence in is information that is clear and not affected or contaminated by your personal stuff. I touched on this earlier, and you may already be familiar with the idea of personal stuff. If you're not, however, I'll briefly go over what that is.

As humans, we have a fairly complex psychology. We have various parts of our mind, including a part that can see and perceive fairly clearly. (This is the part of our consciousness that's unaffected by our personal stuff or transcends it, whether this is connected to our higher soul awareness or not.) We have other parts, however, in which some not-so-clear parts of our awareness reside, such as our fears, entrenched beliefs and mindsets, cultural conditioning, old tapes of negative things we might have been told that play in our minds over and over again, old pain and even abuse, dislikes, and desires and wants. These other parts are what we call personal stuff—and our personal stuff can not only block our ability to perceive things clearly, but it can—and will—contaminate and color our intuitive information. Consider the example of people with a prejudice against other people of certain ethnicities. Anyone with deep-seated dislikes such as this will not be able to see a person of that ethnicity with objectivity—and certainly will not be able to receive clear information about or for the person.

Our personal stuff is not limited to just our fears, wants, etc. It's also true that we're limited by our human mind, which prevents us from perceiving and understanding a range of things beyond our ability to comprehend.

When our personal stuff affects our intuition, *the intuitive information we receive will be suspect and unreliable.*

I cannot stress how important this is. Obviously, the only intuitive information we want is information that is reliable. And if we want reliable information, it's imperative that we bypass our personal stuff. This is no small feat, and it's a pitfall for many people.

Some say that if we're surprised by information we receive, it's likelier to be reliable information. This indeed may be true. It's also true, however, that we can receive information that's reliable and accurate and that doesn't surprise us. Of course, we can also receive information that surprises us and is inaccurate. This makes things a little challenging at times, admittedly.

So how do we ensure that the intuitive information we receive is reliable and not colored by our personal stuff? The method I use and teach, called tuning in, is the best method I know of to try to bypass our personal stuff and not let it color our information. It's not foolproof, but it's the best method that I'm familiar with. We'll be covering that technique in chapter 4, and I highly recommend using it. You want the information you receive to be as reliable as possible.

Intuition Is Highly Individualistic

I know we covered this earlier, but it bears repeating. This is a very important attribute of intuition to know about and keep in mind. Intuition does not work the same way for everyone. Period. It's highly individualistic. That means that yours will be as well. Not keeping this in mind could block you from developing aspects of your intuition.

By allowing your intuition full expression, you may find yourself more surprised and more delighted by it, and this will allow you to develop even more of your potential.

Intuition Can Be Spontaneous or On Demand

Many of us may expect that our intuition will appear to us out of the blue and suddenly speak to us. For example, we may get a gut feeling about something, or a realization may come to us while we're driving. In fact, for most people who haven't developed their intuition, their experiences with intuition usually occur when intuition comes to them spontaneously, seemingly unbidden. Is this the way intuition always presents itself? Do we have to wait for information to come to us?

No, we don't. Fortunately we can also learn how to access our intuition on demand. This is another beauty of intuition: we can experience it either spontaneously or deliberately. Even when information comes to us spontaneously, we may not always recognize it as intuition. This is why we're going over some of the different attributes, forms, and workings of intuition—so you can better recognize it when it appears to you. However, it's indeed a good thing that we can also access information on demand. We'll learn how to do this in chapter 4.

Intuition Works with Your Left Brain

Many people think that they have to choose between their left-brain and right-brain modes. If you're not familiar with these terms, they're easy to understand. They stem from the theory that the two hemispheres of our brain have fairly distinct functions. Left-brain faculties include logic, reasoning, analysis, etc. Right-brain faculties include creativity, feelings, visual imaging, the senses, intuition, perceiving a whole, etc.

Some people feel that you can only be one or the other, either logical or intuitive, for example, and that we need to choose which one to be. I've even heard people say, "I don't think, I feel," or the converse, "I don't feel, I think." This couldn't be further from the truth.

Don't ever limit yourself by feeling that you have to choose between being logical or being intuitive. I personally feel that our brains are designed for the two hemispheres (and modes) to work together synergistically. You're fortunate if you develop and use your intuition, because you can actually use more of your mind that way. Later on, when we look at things to do after receiving intuitive information, you'll see that you actually can and should use your left brain at times when working with your intuition. You can have a mind like a steel trap and be intuitive to boot. Don't ever feel that you have to choose between the two!

Intuition Comes from a Variety of Possible Sources

I've had clients ask over the years where my intuition "comes from." That was something I hadn't even thought about prior to being asked that question the first time. This does bring up an interesting point, and that is that your intuitive information can come from a variety of sources.

Information can come from within you (from the inner workings of your mind), or from outside of you (from guides, the Divine, other people, passed-on loved ones, etc.), or from your body picking up on something. Regardless of where your information is coming from, it's important to trust that it's beneficial and that you're receiving it for a reason.

Try This

After having read about all the different attributes of intuition and the ways in which it can appear, look at the list of your prior intuitive experiences and get a sense of some of the attributes of intuition that you've experienced firsthand. Do you notice that you've experienced several different attributes? Make a note of them in your journal.

What about the sources of the information you've received? Are you sensing that information you've gotten has come from more than one source over the years? Make a note of these as well in your journal.

Are you seeing your intuition now as even more multifaceted than you had realized? Have you allowed your intuition to speak to you in whatever manner it seemed to be presenting itself?

This covers some of the basics of intuition. Intuition has many different facets and presents itself in myriad ways. This information should enable you to better recognize your intuition when it speaks and presents itself to you, so you can take better advantage of its presence and use it as a tool.

Next we'll look at some of the popular myths and misconceptions about intuition, as well as some of its trickier aspects that you'll want to guard against and be aware of.

three

Myths about Intuition and Potential Pitfalls

There are many misconceptions about intuition circulating in our world. This isn't surprising given the fact that intuitive ability is generally not accepted in our culture and, additionally, is so complex. If you don't understand what intuition is and/or you have misconceptions about it, it will be more difficult to recognize and develop your own intuition.

I used to hold many of the common misbeliefs about intuition myself—that is, until I started working with my intuitive sense and delved into it more. As I got further along the path of developing my intuition, I started to see more of the true nature and varied faces of intuition and increasingly understood how far off base these misconceptions were. I also learned from my teaching over the years how much of a block these inaccuracies can be to people in accessing their own intuition. It's very important to address these myths and clear them up, so you can more freely and accurately recognize your own intuition and how it speaks to you, so as to better develop it.

Let's look at some of the popular myths about intuition. I've identified eleven of the more prevalent ones. As we go through them, see if you've been a believer in any of them.

Myths about Intuition

Myth #1

You have to be born with intuitive ability.

We all have the ability and potential to be intuitive. For some people, as we discussed in the last chapter, their intuition is closer to the surface, and they may have more spontaneous experiences with it as a result. However, no matter whether it's closer to the surface or not, just about everyone has intuitive potential and should be able to learn how to harvest intuitive insights on demand, given proper instruction.

In order to access our intuition on demand, we need to shift our state of consciousness. This is something you really can do.

Even if you weren't seeing presences from a young age or predicting the future from the age of two, you are bound to have intuitive potential—and, yes, you can indeed learn how to find your intuition and invite it to speak to you when you'd like.

Intuition is within reach of just about all of us. That's a wonderful thing about intuition, I feel.

Myth #2

It's "women's intuition," and therefore only women have it.

You may have heard it called "women's intuition," but is it really a faculty that belongs just to the estrogen set? Intuition may be called this because women seem to be more accepting of it—or because we've had more prominent examples of women using theirs. Granted, it's a receptive mode (yin), the opposite of men's yang, but this does not mean that it's a faculty that men cannot claim or use.

The truth is that men are just as capable of being intuitive as women. Some men are more naturally intuitive in that they may already be consciously using it, while other men may have to be taught how to find and access theirs— which is the case for many women as well. However, if a man is interested in developing his intuition and is open to it, then he should indeed be able to find his intuition, access it, and develop it. Testosterone is not a block to intuition.

Myth #3

Even if you're intuitive, you have to wait for information to come to you.

No, you don't have to just wait for intuitive information to come to you. We covered this fact in the previous chapter. Even though most people's experience of their intuition might have happened when they spontaneously received intuitive information, you really don't have to wait for information to come to you.

This is one misconception I had myself. I was really surprised to discover, as I felt my way along with my own intuition, that intuitive information could be accessed on demand.

Receiving intuitive information is more a function of setting the tone and inviting it in than just hoping it will come to you. We set the tone by changing our state of consciousness—by tuning in, as I call it. Yes, you will learn specifically how to do this in the next chapter.

Isn't it great that you can learn how to get information on demand?

Myth #4
Intuition works the same way for everyone who is intuitive.

Intuition is definitely not one-size-fits-all. It will vary greatly from one person to the next in how it appears, what it feels like, the forms it comes in, and so forth. Intuition is beautifully individualistic. Each person has his or her own version of intuition.

When you consider this attribute of intuition, you'll realize that it doesn't really matter how it works for someone else. What matters is discovering how it works for *you*. What you want to do is discover what your intuition is like—how it speaks to you and what it feels like. This is one of the things you will start to learn as you go through this book.

How your intuition works is your particular gift, a gift to be valued and honored.

Myth #5

If you're psychic or intuitive, you're omniscient and can know everything.

Wouldn't it be great if you could know everything? Well, unfortunately that's not something we can do, even with our intuition. Many people do feel that being intuitive means that we should be able to get information about anything. However, that's not the case. Intuition is not fail-safe, and using it doesn't mean that you'll be able to know everything.

First of all, our personal stuff, which we discussed in the previous chapter, has great potential to contaminate our information. We can try to bypass it as much as possible, but there's no guarantee that we will be able to do so consistently or completely.

Second, if we're emotionally attached to an issue, it can be very hard to get reliable information about it. We'll be doing some advanced exercises later on that should enable you to be better able to bypass some of your stuff, but that won't guarantee that you'll be able to get accurate information about an issue that is personally important to you—your ailing parent or the romantic relationship you're in, for example.

Third, I personally feel that at times we get the information that we're supposed to have. I feel that we're here on this plane to learn and grow (among other reasons). If we could know everything, we wouldn't be personally unfolding and growing. So if you can't get information about something important to you, please remember that that's likely happening for a reason.

Working with your intuition is more of an art than a science, as I mentioned before. Don't feel that you've failed if you can't get information about everything. That said, you should find yourself improving at your ability to receive quality information that you can trust, even if you can't get information about everything.

Myth #6

If you're intuitive, you can predict the future and therefore avert negative events from happening simply by becoming aware of their imminence.

The truth is that not everyone gets a lot of intuitive information about future events. As we discussed, there are many different types of intuitive information, and different people may tend to get varying types of information. This is perfectly natural.

Negative events happen. That's a sad but true fact of life. When looked at from a different perspective, negative events can often be triggers for our growth and unfolding. I have learned from my intuitive work that if we're supposed to experience something for our own growth, even if it's negative, then even knowing about it in advance may not prevent it from happening. So don't feel bad if you don't get a lot of information about future events or negative ones.

Mystics over the ages—and some people who have had near-death experiences—have said that on the highest levels of the universe there is no time, that all is an "eternal now." In other words, all things and events exist in the present, without a separate past or future. Knowing this may lead you to feel that you should be able to tap into that level, which is somewhat of a repository of all events, both past and future, and get information about the future. This might be true were there not also alternate realities and dimensions, which contemporary theories of science hold to exist. How can you tell which level you've tapped into?

Furthermore, even the most accurate psychics are far from accurate all the time. Taking this into consideration, you can see how difficult it would be to know 100 percent of the time what the future will hold and how to avert a negative event.

Realizing that this is a myth can take a lot of pressure off of you. Don't feel that just because you've developed your intuition, you should always be able to peer into the future and avoid something difficult.

Myth #7
Intuition has no practical applications.

I've always known that this myth isn't true, as do those who use their intuition regularly. If you've ever had an experience with your intuition that helped you in your life (saved you time, prevented an accident, etc.), you know that intuition has practical applications.

Additionally, you'll recall the list of benefits we went over in the introduction. Intuition can aid you in your personal life and at work. It can help us keep any problems in a relationship from getting worse, it can help us to know which direction to take, and it can lead us to make better decisions.

Intuition has myriad practical benefits. Allow yourself to keep your eyes open for more ways in which your intuition can be applied in your life.

Myth #8

There's no rational way to explain intuition, and therefore it's not credible.

Many people believe this, and, indeed, it might have been true many years ago. However, it's not true now. There are several rational ways in which we can explain intuition at present, from mechanisms in our mind, to contemporary theories in physics, to research on additional human senses, to spiritual explanations.

Suffice it to say that there are now several ways in which we can explain intuition, and advances in both science and awareness are yielding even more. We're living in a wonderful time, when more and more things are being shown to us about intuition and increasing numbers of people are embracing it, developing it, and claiming it as their own.

Myth #9

Intuition is foolproof.

Many people do feel that intuition is foolproof. However, this is not true. Intuition is so complex and involved that we just can't say that it's foolproof. Consider, for example, how your personal stuff can contaminate the intuitive information you get. From that standpoint alone, you can see how your intuition may not always be foolproof or reliable all the time.

Additionally, as I mentioned under myth #5, I feel that we get the information we're supposed to have. This means that we may get information that's not accurate in order for us to experience something we're supposed to experience, for our unfolding.

Another reason why it's true that intuition is not fool-proof is that some of the information we receive may need to be interpreted, and interpretation of the information we get can definitely leave room for error.

In spite of intuition not always being foolproof, it's still quite valuable and can give us many gifts once we learn how to work with it. Over time, you may be able to discern which pieces of information feel more reliable than others.

Myth #10
Intuition is only for spiritual, mystical, or New Agey people.

Intuition is definitely not just for those who are spiritual. Because most of us have the potential to be intuitive and use our intuition, being spiritual is not a prerequisite.

There are many businesspeople (both male and female) who use their intuition, even if they call it a hunch or gut feeling. (Of course, businesspeople can also be spiritual.)

It truly doesn't take a spiritual orientation to unlock intuitive potential or to use intuition expertly, nor do you need to subscribe to New Age ideas in order to find your intuition and develop it. Intuition is really democratic. It's not a private club, and you don't need to sign anything or pay dues to use it.

Myth #11
Intuitive people are illogical (or flaky or lacking in intelligence).

There's a popular stereotype of intuitive people as being illogical. However, it's just that—a stereotype.

In chapter 2, we covered the fact that you can use your whole brain. In other words, you can use your left brain (logic) and your right brain (creativity and intuition). The two are not mutually exclusive, no matter how much our cultural thinking these days is swayed toward feeling that we have to choose between the two. This means that you can be both logical and intuitive and that using your intuition doesn't mean that you can't also be logical. You don't have to choose between the two! You can have and use both.

One beauty of developing your intuition is that it actually gives you more mental resources to use in your life. As complicated and stressful as our lives can be these days, that's truly a good thing.

Try This

Now that you've read the eleven myths I've identified about intuition, can you think of any more that weren't listed?

Do any of the eleven myths resonate with you? Have you thought that any of them were true? If so, can you now see (and accept) that they're inaccurate?

As you do some of the exercises later in the book, allow yourself to review these misconceptions and see if you find yourself realizing even more the reasons why they're fallacies.

Potential Pitfalls to Be Aware of

I wish I could promise you that working with your intuition will always be smooth sailing, but that won't necessarily be the case. There are some potential pitfalls you'll want to be on the lookout for. It's better for you to be aware of these pitfalls now, rather than finding out midstream that you've gotten ensnared in one.

We've discussed some of these potential problems before, so they likely won't come as a surprise to you. Let's look at how you might avoid getting caught by any of them.

Expecting That You Can Know Everything

You'll recall that being intuitive doesn't mean that you'll become omniscient. In all likelihood, you'll encounter topics that you may not be able to get information about.

So what should you do?

I would suggest, first of all, that you take the pressure off of yourself. Remind yourself that as much as you would like to feel that you can access information on anything, you more than likely won't be able to. That means that it's not a failing if you can't.

If you're trying to get intuitive information on something and find yourself waiting and waiting, with no information coming in, allow yourself to stop and take a mini-break. Remind yourself that this may be an instance in which the information will elude you. You can always tune back in and try again. However, if the information still doesn't come in, then allow yourself to remember that you won't be able to get information on everything.

You could try to rephrase your question or even to access information on a different aspect of the topic—and you might succeed. However, if you still find yourself without the information you're seeking, give yourself a break. Remind yourself that you haven't failed. Instead, you've just encountered a subject for which the information is currently inaccessible. That can happen at times to even the best of professional intuitives.

Interpreting Intuitive Information Incorrectly

We can get all types of intuitive information, and, as we've covered, some of the information may not be literal. It may be symbolic instead. Knowing what to do with symbolic information can be another potential pitfall because the first thing we need to do is interpret that information correctly.

So what do you do if you've received information that doesn't seem straightforward?

The first thing to do is to start working on interpreting it. If it's information for something you want to know about, start by asking yourself, "What could this mean to me?" If it's information you've gotten for someone else, ask that person that same question, while also seeing if you intuitively have a sense of the meanings. You can also try to free-associate with the symbolic information.

Remember that you can bring your intuition into this exercise as well. Does your interpretation of the symbolic information feel right or not?

If you've worked at interpreting the information over and over again and you find yourself stymied, take a break. Do something else for a while. You may find that the right interpretation (the one that feels right) will pop into your mind after you've walked away and focused on something else, or even the next day or a few days later. Just because you find yourself having a difficult time interpreting information at times doesn't mean that you'll never be able to interpret symbolic information. Taking a break often can help.

Interpreting symbolic information is not a straightforward process, and, of course, gleaning the correct interpretation will be critical to being able to productively use the intuitive information you've received, when it's symbolic. This is a pitfall, but one that you can learn to work with.

Receiving Intentionally Inaccurate Information

This is a tough one to deal with. When we receive information, we often don't know whether it's accurate or is actually information that we're supposed to get and believe.

You could do additional exercises that allow you to question what you received. The "Yes/No" exercise we'll be doing in chapter 6 is one of them. You can ask yourself if the information feels right. You can also wait several days to see if the information still resonates. You could also tune in again in a few days or weeks to see if you receive the same information. However, if you are indeed supposed to get the information, even if it's not correct, then there may not be much you can do. The truth is that you may receive information from time to time that isn't accurate but that you're supposed to feel is accurate. (This tends to be the exception when receiving intuitive information rather than the rule. So it probably won't happen very often.)

Why would this be the case? If we're supposed to experience something in our lives for our own personal process, then despite our best efforts to the contrary, events may unfold that lead us to experience it, regardless of the information we've received or tried to check out that may have led us not to experience it.

Separating True Intuitive Information from Our Personal Stuff

This is another tough pitfall to deal with. The method I use and teach to access intuition—tuning in—can help with this. However, nothing is truly fail-safe when it comes to working with intuition.

Learning to be clear with ourselves can also help, but this is very difficult for us to do. We are spiritual beings, but our human side usually gets in the way of our clarity, especially if we don't try to guard against it happening. Having clarity with ourselves comes from learning to observe ourselves objectively and from what's called "living consciously" (observing our own behavior as if we were someone else). Meditation also helps us to see more clearly within ourselves—into our motivations, fears, wants, etc.—which can lead to our being clearer with ourselves.

The more we're able to see objectively into our own depths, including our own personal stuff, the clearer we'll be with ourselves. And the clearer we are with ourselves, the better we'll be able to sense if our personal stuff is contaminating the intuitive information we receive.

This is a process. We don't acquire the ability overnight to separate out our personal stuff from intuitive information. However, it's something we can definitely work on.

Having clarity and clear perception as a goal is an admirable one and one that we can indeed move toward and improve upon.

Try This

Allow yourself to look over the potential pitfalls we just explored. Can you identify any of your past intuitive experiences where you may have faced any of them? Can you see a way to work with them now that you couldn't see then? Make some notes in your journal about your insights.

In this chapter we covered multiple misconceptions about intuition and some potential pitfalls that you'll want to be on the lookout for and avoid. This information amplifies all the ins and outs of intuition that we previously examined. All of this is preparing you to work with your intuition more effectively.

You've no doubt had spontaneous experiences with your intuition in the past. How can you begin to access it on demand? This is what we'll turn our attention to next.

How Do You Access
Your Intuition?

You're probably beginning to see how your intuition works. This is a good thing! Now we're going to get into the nitty-gritty of how we actually access our intuition and can better receive information, whether through tuning in or through it appearing spontaneously.

I've mentioned to you before that I use and teach the method of tuning in. This is a method to access intuition on demand. Intuitive information can also come to us spontaneously, as you know. Even though information can come to us spontaneously, we might not always be aware of it having come in or know how to improve the chances of it coming to us.

Irrespective of whether we're getting information spontaneously or on demand, there's a state of mind that helps with both. We need to be in a more relaxed state of mind in order to access intuition. In other words, we need a slower brain wave pattern than we may be in most of the time while we're awake.

What do I mean by a slower brain wave pattern? You may already be familiar with brain waves, but in case you aren't, we'll go over some basics. Our brains produce different types of brain waves, which are measured by an electroencephalogram, and these various brain waves help to produce different states of consciousness. Brain waves vary in wave frequency, amplitude, and volume. The four main types of brain waves are, from faster to slowest, beta, alpha, theta, and delta. (Gamma brain waves also exist and are the fastest, but they usually occur briefly, during moments of insight.) Here's a brief rundown on the four main brain wave types and their typical correlating states of consciousness:

- Beta brain waves—Being alert, focused on a task, worrying or being stressed
- Alpha brain waves—Daydreaming, stream of consciousness, calmness, creativity
- Theta brain waves—The subconscious, prominent during meditation and falling asleep, receptivity
- Delta brain waves—The unconscious, largely prominent during the deeper levels of sleep, and a type of inner radar

Normally, in our fast-paced society, we'll predominantly be in a beta brain wave state while we're awake, especially if we're stressed. When we relax and even allow ourselves to daydream and let our mind wander, we'll find ourselves in a more relaxed—and slower—brain wave state, that of alpha. In lighter levels of sleep, we'll be in theta, and in delta in the deepest levels of sleep. This is admittedly a simplification, as at any one time we usually have all four brain waves present in different proportions.

Keeping in mind what I said about needing to be in a more relaxed state of mind in order to access our intuition, you can guess that we'll need to be in more of an alpha brain wave state.

Even though we want to be in that more relaxed state of mind to access both spontaneous and on-demand intuition, the procedures to do that and the states of consciousness involved are slightly different from one other.

Let's start by looking at how we access spontaneous intuitive information—or, I should say, how we increase the likelihood of receiving intuitive information spontaneously.

Accessing Your Intuition Spontaneously

Accessing intuitive information spontaneously can feel like a gift. It's easy. You don't have to work at anything. Something just comes to you and—voilà!—there it is for you, intuitive information. Information can appear to you as a thought, a fleeting image, a feeling, or in other forms. Regardless of how it appears to you, the information is just suddenly there. We can't make that happen, since it happens spontaneously, but we can increase the likelihood of it occurring, as well as of our consciously registering the information.

Before we look at how we can do that, we need to know that intuitive information can come to us spontaneously in different ways. Basically, those ways include the following three:

1. Something pops into your mind while you're awake.
2. Your body may register information (the bodily awareness, or embodied cognition, that we touched on earlier in chapter 2).
3. Information may come to you while you're sleeping, in the sleep or dream state.

Let's look at what we need to do in each of these scenarios.

Spontaneously Knowing Something While Awake

This is really fairly simple to do. You want to be in a relaxed state of mind, notably alpha, from time to time. The best way to get a sense of what it feels like to be in an alpha state of mind is to think of what it feels like when you're daydreaming. Daydreaming is like a stream of consciousness in which your mind is unfettered and effortlessly flows from one subject to another.

You may have been told at some point that daydreaming is a waste of time. However, quite the opposite is true. Daydreaming serves a very useful purpose. Interestingly, research in the past few years has shown that alpha, or daydreaming, is the "default setting" of the mind. In other words, if we're not focused on a specific task while we're awake, our minds tend to automatically turn to daydreaming, or alpha.

So why is alpha, or daydreaming, important here? As you'll recall, some intuitive information can come from deeper within our minds, as opposed to from outside of us all the time. (Of course, a lot of our intuitive information does indeed come from outside of us.) You'll also recall that intuition is a receptive mode, a receiving of information.

If you're focused on a task and concentrating on it, you are not in the receptive mode necessary to receive information or to notice it when it comes in. It takes an alpha state of mind (daydreaming) for us to be open enough to receive and notice information. This is why that state of mind is so important for receiving intuitive information spontaneously.

Needless to say, you don't want to be daydreaming all the time. You'd never get any work done. You want to allow yourself to be in alpha (or daydreaming) *some* of the time, but not *all* of the time or *none* of the time.

Simply daydreaming, however, is not the end of the story or all that you need to do in order to receive intuitive information spontaneously. It's just the first part. The second part is that, while you're daydreaming, you want to observe what's going through your mind. Awareness of your thoughts is how you catch those insights and all the intuitive information coming to you spontaneously. It can be that simple.

That said, however, if you're stressed a lot of the time, you may find that you hardly ever daydream or get into that relaxed, alpha state of mind. Stress is not good for your health or for accessing intuitive information spontaneously. So the first thing you want to do, if you want to increase the chances of your receiving intuitive information spontaneously, is to address your stress. You can do this by either reducing your exposure to stress or, if that is hard to do, getting some stress relief. There are many different ways to de-stress, including taking a relaxing bath, exercising, engaging in a hobby you enjoy, and socializing with friends. You will know yourself which activities are relaxing for you.

Tuning in, the method we'll be learning later in this chapter to access information on demand, can also help with stress, as it's slightly meditative. (In fact, meditation in and of itself will also help greatly with stress relief.)

Stress aside, in order to optimize your receiving intuitive information spontaneously, you'll want to take advantage of those times when you find yourself daydreaming, which means you'll want to identify when that occurs. I have found that some of the best times—and most likely times—in which we'll find ourselves daydreaming are when we're performing routine activities, those somewhat mindless tasks that we do on a fairly regular basis that don't require full attention or concentration. These can include your daily habits, such as taking a shower, washing the dishes, exercising, brushing your teeth, etc. Lots of insights may come to you then.

In order to access intuitive information spontaneously, you'll want to do what you can to make it more likely to happen and for you to notice the information coming in. You can do this by allowing your mind to wander from time to time—and then, while you're daydreaming, by paying attention to what's going through your mind.

One note on this, though: information that comes to you while daydreaming can leave just as quickly. So when information comes to you spontaneously and you notice it coming in, you'll want to make a note of it, at least mentally if not also literally writing it down. You won't be happy to lose useful insights. This would be an excellent time for you to use your journal and jot those insights down.

Try This

Allow yourself to think of experiences you've had in the past in which you received intuitive information. Did some of it come to you spontaneously?

Can you remember a time when intuitive information did come to you spontaneously? If so, what frame of mind were you in when that happened? Did you make a mental note of the information? Can you remember having intuitive information coming to you and then forgetting afterward what it was? Make a note in your journal of each of these.

Accessing and Using Information Your Body Registers

Your body, as you've learned, can also intuitively pick up on things quite spontaneously and effortlessly. In fact, we don't usually have conscious control over our body registering something. It just happens. Your body picks up on information all of a sudden without your willing it to happen. You may notice that you suddenly have goose bumps, or your stomach may suddenly feel funny, or your heart may feel warm and pleasant all of a sudden. With my Katrina experience, I kept noticing that I was feeling somewhat sick to my stomach.

Even though your body can pick up on something, at the same time you can often be completely unaware consciously of what that information is. Normally, missing out on the information won't be much of a problem. However, there are instances in which people are picking up on negative information and the not knowing can be problematic. There are many people who suffer from irritable bowel syndrome (IBS) or other chronic stomach issues, and I personally wonder if some of them may be experiencing this. (Of course, for many people with IBS, the problem stems from the food being eaten.) It could be that some people with IBS, however, are picking up on negative information via their gut, and it may create a physical problem for them because they are consciously unaware of what the information is, while the information "eats" at them unconsciously. The disconnect between their conscious awareness and what their gut is registering could result in physical symptoms that can persist.

In situations like these, being able to consciously know what your gut is picking up on can even be beneficial for your health. In addition to helping you address health concerns, being able to consciously glean what your body is picking up on can be helpful to you in other ways.

How can you become aware of the information that is coming through your body without your having any idea as to what it is?

First of all, pay attention to your body, so you will notice when it's registering something. Pay attention if parts of your body suddenly feel different, such as sudden goose bumps or a sudden light feeling in your heart, rather than dismissing them or ignoring them.

Once you've noticed that a part of your body seems to be registering something, you'll want to find a way to determine what it is that's being registered. This can be easier said than done without a guide as to how to go about it.

Fortunately, there's a way you can do this. Just as some people find a way to communicate with animals and even the earth and trees, for example, so too can you communicate with your body.

Here's a procedure you can use to consciously access the information that your body has picked up on spontaneously.

Body Communication Procedure

1. Identify the part of your body that is sensing something.
2. Close your eyes.
3. Take a few deep breaths until you feel yourself relaxed.
4. Keep breathing more deeply than normal while you clear your mind.
5. Visualize the part of your body that appears to be intuitively picking up on information—for example, your gut.
6. Call your body part by name while visualizing it—by saying, for example, "Hello, gut."
7. Ask the part of your body what it wants to tell you or what it's picking up on—for example, "What

would you like to tell me?" or "What is it that you're sensing?"

8. Observe what comes into your mind, no matter what it is or which form it comes in, as well as how you feel, both emotionally and in your body.

9. If you feel yourself getting distracted or starting to heed what is going on outside of you (noises, other distractions, etc.), or if you feel that no information has come in, start the process over again.

10. Thank the part of your body for its information, partnership with you, and willingness to assist you.

This is a pretty simple procedure, isn't it? It should be easy to follow, as long as you allow yourself to get into that more relaxed and deeper state of consciousness. The exercises we'll be doing later in the book should help you to do that even more.

You can use this procedure any time you sense that your body has picked up on information that you'd like to make conscious.

Accessing Information from the Sleep and Dream States

Intuitive information can also come to us spontaneously in the sleep and dream states. Trying to be in an alpha state of consciousness when this occurs obviously won't work given that we're sleeping. How can we consciously access that information so we can take advantage of what it's giving us?

There are two different ways we can do this, depending on whether the information has come to us in a dream or in non-dreaming sleep.

Many people believe that if intuitive information comes to us while we're asleep, it will only come in dreams. That's not true. We can also gain insights and receive information while we're sleeping and not dreaming, although bringing that information back to our conscious awareness can be challenging. Usually when we wake up, any traces of insight from our sleeping mind and sleeping "awareness" seem to quickly dissipate, like wisps of smoke dispersing and disappearing.

Even though consciously grasping these insights can be challenging, we can optimize the possibility of our glimpsing, remembering, and retaining those gifts of intuitive information. The best way to do that is to allow yourself to wake up slowly, gradually coming back to conscious awareness. As you do this, watch what is going through your mind as you luxuriate in allowing yourself to savor any morsels appearing to you. This truly is the best way to capture those insights.

Unfortunately, in our fast-paced society, many people jolt awake to the jarring sound of an alarm clock, whether it makes a loud noise or plays music. After jolting awake, they jump out of bed and hit the ground running. If you do this, you can forget about bringing any insights and intuitive information back with you. That information will likely be gone, and it can be very challenging to try to get it back.

If you want to capture and take advantage of intuitive information that came to you while sleeping, allow yourself to slowly come back to waking consciousness and make light mental notes of any information and insights going through your mind. Write them down in your journal as well. Yes, you may have to allot more time to your morning routine, but it will be well worth it. You may be surprised by what was given to you during your sleep state and how helpful it can be.

What about dreams? As you know, dreams are often a rich source of intuitive information. It can be so beneficial to mine the richness of our dreams for the intuitive information (as well as other types of information) they contain and can give us. One reality of our dreams, however, is that they often are so full of symbols that their meanings can escape us. In fact, many people don't pay attention to their intuitive and psychic dreams because they don't understand them. They feel that their dreams just seem bizarre because of all the symbols in them and seemingly strange scenarios.

The good thing is that we can indeed learn how to interpret our dreams, allowing us to consciously understand them and use them as a tool in our lives. You can learn how to decode your dreams and derive their meanings and gifts for yourself, and the information on dreams in the appendix should give you a good jumpstart on that.

You are probably getting a lot of intuitive and psychic information in your dreams, along with some other useful information. There's no reason not to take advantage of it. If you feel that you don't dream, know that everyone does, in fact, dream, unless there's a brain abnormality or other problem. If you're sleep-deprived, you'll likely be spending more time in the deeper levels of sleep, where we tend to have fewer dreams and tend not to remember those we do have.

Even if you're not sleep-deprived, you may still be dreaming, even in the lighter levels of sleep (where most dreams occur), and still not be remembering your dreams. We tend to remember our dreams only when our level of consciousness shifts while we're dreaming, usually because there's a slight noise, or we shift position, etc. So if you're sleeping "through" your dreams without any awakening or shift in consciousness, you may not remember them.

It's also true that some people simply are not motivated to remember their dreams. If this describes you and you now feel that you want to remember your dreams, know that you can train your mind to signal you when you're dreaming. First of all, you'll need to remind yourself that you want to remember your dreams—and then give yourself a pre-sleep suggestion that you want to do that. When you go to bed, just remind yourself before going to sleep, "I want to remember my dreams." It may take a while, but over time you should find yourself remembering more of your dreams.

I should also add that I don't recommend working with every dream you have. Some dreams really aren't significant or aren't giving us important intuitive information or other insights. While there's no hard and fast rule to follow, we usually know when a dream is significant—because we may feel for some reason that it's significant, or we may have trouble putting it out of our minds, or it keeps echoing through our minds the next day, or it scares us or even elates us. You could drive yourself crazy trying to write down and figure out every dream you have, so make it easier on yourself by focusing only on the ones you sense are significant.

We can get a lot out of our dreams. They can give us some wonderful gifts—those insights and intuitive information. So remember to wake up slowly, use your journal to jot down insights and dreams, get enough sleep, and read the information in the appendix on interpreting dreams.

You now know how to better access your intuition and remember information when it speaks to you spontaneously. Next we'll look at how to access intuition on demand.

Accessing Your Intuition on Demand

This is what many people would like to be able to do with their intuition—access it on demand and be able to get intuitive information whenever they wish. I personally feel that this is something we can all learn how to do, given certain bounds and limitations on the information itself—such as that we won't be able to know everything, for example.

How can you access your intuition on demand? I use, recommend, and teach the method of tuning in, and that is what we're going to go over next.

Tuning In

Tuning in is a method by which you close your eyes, go to a deeper level of consciousness, and receive intuitive information. By a deeper level of consciousness, I mean a more relaxed state of consciousness (as we discussed earlier in the section on brain wave states). However, this is not a light alpha state of mind, which we talked about for accessing spontaneous information. This is a deeper level of consciousness with slower brain waves than that. It's closer to meditation than to daydreaming. If you've never meditated before, you'll get some practice with this in the next chapter.

Before I share the procedure for tuning in, I'd like you to know that there's a reason why you're supposed to close your eyes while doing it. Whenever we close our eyes and start breathing more deeply, we gradually lose our orientation to what is outside of us and around us and shift our orientation to what is inside of us. This is very important in working with your intuition. Focusing on what's going on around you or being distracted by external sounds, lights, etc., will interfere with your ability to receive intuitive information. So allow yourself to close your eyes whenever you tune in.

Another thing you need to know before we go over the procedure for tuning in is how to prepare to receive intuitive information—whether you should do any special preparation or not. We'll be discussing this in more detail in chapter 10, but I'll share a little bit with you here.

How you prepare to get intuitive information is really a matter of personal preference. There's no one right way to prepare before tuning in. Over time, as you gain more experience with your intuition, you may create your own way to prepare. For example, you may want to light some candles or say a prayer or even visualize guides. This is not necessary or required for you to be able to tune in. However, some people may feel better if they set the stage, so to speak. If you live your life in a prayerful way, with a spiritual awareness and orientation, you may not need to do any additional preparation. Maintaining a spiritual attitude can keep us in a good place and predispose us to tapping into wisdom and intuitive information quite easily. However, as I said, how you prepare—or indeed whether you prepare in any way at all—is purely a matter of personal preference. You may read or hear of ways that other people use to prepare, but you will be the one to know what you want or need to do.

If you're receiving intuitive information for someone else, you may want to remind yourself that you want to be helpful to the person—or even say a prayer, asking to be given beneficial information. Doing something like this certainly won't hurt and may even serve as a reminder that accessing intuitive information in a situation like this is meant to benefit another and is not about our own abilities or ego. I often say a prayer, asking that I be given information that will be helpful to my client.

One more note: I've had some people express concern over the years about what they're tapping into, out of fear of having negative energies affect them or of information coming from a negative source. I know that this is a real concern for many people. I, however, have never personally been concerned about this. I've always felt a connection to the Divine and felt guided and protected. I feel that if you trust that this is a benevolent universe and you allow yourself to connect to positive energies, this will become less of a fear for you. Connecting with the Divine and positive energies keeps us protected.

If you feel that it will help you to imagine or visualize that your information is coming from a specific source (God, guides, an angel, even a knowledgeable person, etc.), that's fine. However, don't tell yourself that you can only receive information from that source or that you can only receive certain types of information.

Now let's take a look at how we actually tune in. Assume for this procedure that you have already set the stage through your preparation procedure and conducted any procedure for protecting yourself, if you feel that either is necessary for you. For now, realize that this is a procedure for you to have as a guideline and not an exercise for you to do at this point. You'll use and apply it in some of the later exercises, so you may want to bookmark this page.

Procedure for Tuning In to Receive Intuitive Information

1. Identify the intuitive information you'd like to receive.
2. Close your eyes.
3. Take a few deep breaths until you feel yourself relaxing.
4. Keep breathing more deeply than normal while you clear your mind.
5. Pose the question you have and then wait. (If you want to visualize your information coming from a certain source, this is where you can do that.)
6. Observe what comes into your mind, no matter what it is, as well as how you feel, both emotionally and in your body.
7. If you feel yourself getting distracted or starting to heed what is going on outside of you (noises, other distractions, etc.), start the process over again.

That is how you tune in. Tuning in is admittedly easier for those who have meditated before. In the next chapter, we'll be doing some preliminary intuitive exercises, the first of which is a meditation. So whether you've meditated before or not, you'll get some practice soon.

Note that the first step you take for tuning in is to identify the information you'd like to receive. This is so that you can set your "inner antenna," so it knows what type of information you're seeking. You can also opt to receive open-ended information. In this case, you could say, for example, "I'd like to receive information that will be helpful to me in my life at the present time." Identifying what you'd like your inner antenna to focus on truly helps.

When you clear your mind, you'll want to make sure that your normal internal mind chatter has stopped. It's by stopping the mind chatter that you allow true intuitive information to come to your awareness. This can take some practice.

You can use this procedure for tuning in whenever you'd like to access your intuition—in other words, whenever there's something you'd like to know more about. It allows you to be in the driver's seat a little more with your intuition, instead of waiting around for information to come to you spontaneously. I've never had anyone not be able to get information with this procedure. However, it can take practice. So you'll definitely want to work with it on a regular basis and get more and more practice. If you do, you should find yourself improving at receiving intuitive information. You should find yourself able to do this at will!

Try This

Allow yourself to think of something you've had on your mind, something you want to get some information on. Once you've identified it, allow yourself to tune in, using the procedure just described, and see what comes to you.

If you tune in for the first time and feel that no information has come to you, wait a few hours and try the procedure again.

Make a note in your journal of what you've experienced.

Now think back to intuitive experiences you've had in the past. What state of mind were you in when intuitive information came to you? Were you actually tuning in at any time in the past when you received information, whether you did so deliberately or not?

five

Meditation Exercises
to Enter an Intuitive State

Now that you've explored the basics of intuition, as well as how to access your intuition on demand and consciously register information that has come to you spontaneously, the next thing to do is to go through some exercises to give you practice in developing your own intuitive abilities. The ones we'll do in this chapter are designed to allow you to experience a state of consciousness conducive to intuition and receiving information. In the next chapter, you'll find some beginner exercises that will give you practice in receiving intuitive information in different ways.

Some of these exercises will be open-ended, in the sense of not trying to get intuitive information about a specific topic or question, while others in the next chapter will be focused on receiving information about something specific. For the open-ended ones, just allow yourself to see what comes to you.

Here are some things to keep in mind before doing the exercises, both in this chapter and the next one:

- No matter what you experience, try to accept it, no matter how strange it may seem at the time.

- Be on the lookout for your left brain interrupting and trying to censor what's happening, especially during the meditations. If you find yourself thinking, "What am I supposed to experience?" or "Maybe I'm making this up," just ignore it. Allow yourself to go with whatever you're experiencing in the exercise.

- Remember that some of these exercises are open-ended, and there's nothing specific you're supposed to experience.

- If you know other people who are doing these exercises, either with you or by themselves, don't compare your experience with theirs, when you share things, in a way that leads you to feel you should have experienced similar things. This is highly individualistic. What you experience is what you're supposed to experience, especially during the meditations.

- If you do these exercises with someone else, allow yourself to compare notes after each one and validate each other's experience. Being able to see what someone else has experienced can allow you to learn more about intuition and its possibilities. In addition, you may see significance in what the other person experienced that he or she hadn't grasped—and vice versa. However, as you share things, don't compare yourself with anyone else.

- *Don't get discouraged!* Working with your intuition is an art and takes practice. As you continue to do intuitive exercises, preferably on a regular basis if you're serious about developing your intuition, you should see improvement over time.

- You may find more information coming to you after you've finished doing an exercise, even a day or week afterward. So remember that more information could come to you later. Sometimes in doing intuitive exercises, and especially with meditations, we experience shifts in energy, and when we do, we often find more information coming to our awareness during the next few days or weeks following the exercise (or shift).

- Pay attention to your dreams after doing these exercises, as more information may come to you while you're sleeping.

- Try to do these exercises without expecting anything in particular to happen—and try to suspend any judgment about the exercises or how you do with them. No matter what you experience, it should be worthwhile and happening for a reason.

- Some exercises may feel easier to you than others. This is natural and nothing to be concerned about. If an exercise feels a little too hard for you, stop doing it and don't judge yourself. You can always go back to it later and try it again, perhaps after a few days or a week.

- Remember to turn off your phone and television and any other potential sources of noise. You don't want to be interrupted during the exercises, especially during the meditations. If you're interrupted or distracted while doing an exercise, especially a meditation, it may take some time to get back to where you were. Instead, you may need to start the exercise over again from the beginning.

- If you find that you didn't receive any information during or after the exercises, remember that this may be a time when you're not supposed to know certain things. Repeat the exercise and see if information comes in. If it still doesn't, then maybe you are not supposed to have an answer at this time.

- Take your time doing the exercises. They're not timed and you don't need to rush with them.

Bear in mind that your intuition is like a treasure chest, and you may not be aware of all the treasure that's in it until you begin to open it. Approach these exercises with pleasant excitement, but without any expectations or imposed restrictions.

Because the method I use and teach to access intuitive information is that of tuning in, which you learned about in the last chapter, I always start with meditative exercises, as they will allow you to get into a deeper level of consciousness.

Meditation in and of itself can provide us with many different benefits, both physical and psychological. I not only meditate myself, but I also use guided meditation as a modality in my private work with clients. I've seen first-hand the magic that meditation, especially customized guided meditation, can work and the inner shifts it can bring about, along with shifts in energy. If you want to move some energy on a topic or issue close to you, just try meditation, especially a customized guided meditation.

Meditation is good not only for its inner benefits but also for its health benefits. The benefit that most people are aware of is stress relief, but that is just the tip of the iceberg. Meditation can also lower blood pressure, allow you to focus and concentrate better, decrease any anxiety or worry, reduce depression, improve your mood, improve your memory—well, there's a long list of benefits, and I still read regularly about new research finding additional health benefits.

Regular meditation can also help us be clearer in our perception and see some of our personal issues more clearly. As a result, meditation can help us get clearer intuitive information.

If you haven't meditated before and if you're concerned that a meditative state will be hard for you to get into, don't worry. The exercises we'll be doing in this chapter are a form of meditation called *guided meditation*, which tends to be fairly easy to get into. You won't need to make your mind go blank. Instead, you'll be guided through the meditation. You can either record the meditations yourself and then play them back, or you can go to my website at www .dianebrandon.com and purchase the audio downloads.

Please start with this Initial Guided Meditation! It's very important that you do this guided meditation first.

Exercise: Initial Guided Meditation

This first meditation should enable you to get into that deeper level of consciousness where you'll find it easier to access intuitive information. You'll notice that there are places in the meditation with an ellipsis (…). Whenever you see an ellipsis, allow yourself to pause and take some extra time. You can take extra time anywhere you'd like in the meditation if you're still experiencing things and not ready to move on. If you're using a recording, just pause the recording whenever this happens.

Sit or lie down. Make sure you get as physically comfortable as you can. Close your eyes. Start taking some deep breaths, and feel that you're relaxing more and more each time you exhale. If any part of your body feels tight or sore, feel your breath going to those sore or tight places as you inhale. Then, as you exhale, feel that you're exhaling that soreness or tightness.

Allow yourself to continue breathing deeply, knowing that you're taking this time just for yourself. Allow yourself to enjoy this time, with no sense of obligation or concern about things you need to do. This is your time just for yourself.

As you continue to breathe deeply, relaxing more and more, allow yourself to feel your body sinking into the chair, floor, bed, or whatever you're sitting or lying on. Feel your body letting go more and more, and relaxing….

Now allow yourself to find a breathing pattern that's a little deeper than usual, but not so deep that it's labored.... As you do this, allow yourself to focus your attention on your feet, on your toes—and now feel your toes let go and relax.

Now feel the relaxation in your toes start to move up your feet, as if it had a mind of its own. Feel that relaxation moving through the arches of your feet and then into your ankles, relaxing everything as it goes along.

Now feel that relaxation moving into your legs— the calves of your legs. You might experience it as a pleasant tingling or slight warmth. Feel your calves relax. Feel that relaxation still inching its way upward.

Now feel it in your knees, and feel them relax and let go. Feel that relaxation now moving up from your knees into your thighs.... Feel those muscles relax. Now feel that relaxation move into your pelvic area, and feel the relaxation there.

Now feel that relaxation move into your stomach. Feel all the muscles in your stomach loosening their hold and relaxing so there's no tension whatsoever in your stomach.

Now allow yourself to take a deep, deep breath in, and as you exhale that breath, feel yourself completely relaxed all the way from your stomach, down your legs, and out through your toes....

Now find that comfortable breathing pattern once again and focus your attention on your stomach and the relaxation there. Feel that relaxation starting to move upward again, now moving into your solar plexus, the area right above your stomach. Feel your solar plexus relax.

Now feel that relaxation move into your lower chest.... Feel the relaxation there. Now feel it move upward into your heart area, and feel your heart relax and open, like petals of a flower unfurling. You might also feel a pleasant glow in your heart area.

Feel that relaxation moving upward again, now moving into your upper chest. Now feel it move out laterally in each direction, and feel your shoulders drop and relax. Feel that relaxation moving down each arm—down through your upper arms, your elbows, your forearms, your wrists, your hands, and your fingers.... Feel your arms completely relaxed....

Now take another deep, deep breath in, and as you inhale, feel that breath filling up your arms with air so they expand in size. Then as you exhale, feel your arms contract to normal size.... Do that one more time, inhaling and your arms growing in size, then exhaling and your arms contracting to normal size again....

Focus your attention now on the relaxation in your upper chest, and feel it starting to move upward again, now moving into your throat. Feel your throat relax, perhaps even feeling a pleasant warmth there....

Feel that relaxation moving now into your jaw, and feel your jaw just drop and let go—no tightness whatsoever there.

Now feel that relaxation moving up into your mouth, and feel your mouth relax. Now feel it moving upward again, into your nose and cheeks. You might even feel a pleasant glow in your cheeks....

Now feel it moving upward into your eyes. Feel them relax. Feel it moving upward into your eyebrows. Feel them relax....

Now feel the relaxation moving upward into your forehead. Feel all the muscles there letting go and relaxing so there are no lines in your forehead....

Now feel that relaxation moving upward into the top of your head, the crown area. Feel it relax. You might also feel a glow or warmth there....

Now allow yourself to feel that you're completely relaxed, all the way from the top of your head, down your body, and out through your toes....

Take a deep, deep breath in, and feel your body expand in size. Then exhale and feel your body contract in size. Allow yourself to do that one more time, inhaling and expanding in size, and exhaling and contracting back to normal size....

Allow yourself once again to find that comfortable breathing pattern, and allow yourself to realize that you're getting ready to go on a journey. You don't know where you're going yet, but that's fine. Allow yourself to enjoy this pleasant sense of getting ready to go on a journey.

Now see or feel yourself walking down a hallway. You're in no rush to get anywhere. You're just walking down this hallway. As you walk along, you find yourself looking to your right and to your left at the walls where there are pictures—pictures of different scenes, different places. You're just walking along slowly, looking at these pictures, feeling the temperature in here, noticing any ambient sounds, any odors or fragrances.

Some of these pictures really pull your attention, and you want to look at them a little longer. Others you may just glance at and move on....

You continue walking down this hallway, enjoying the sense of not having to be anywhere—just leisurely walking along. You notice that there's a door at the end of the hallway, but you're in no rush to get there.

You continue walking along, noticing which pictures pull your attention, noticing that you're getting closer to the door at the end of the hallway. Still walking along....

You now find yourself at the end of the hallway standing in front of that door. Allow yourself to look at the door. What color is it? What is it made of? What type of doorknob or handle does it have?

You realize that you want to go through this door, so you reach out and grab the handle. You open the door, and as it opens you feel some slightly cooler air on your face. You notice that the light is a little dimmer on the other side.

You now walk through the doorway, and you find yourself on a landing with several steps going down. You know you want to go down these steps, so you start walking down them—feeling more and more relaxed as you go down, knowing that you're getting closer to where you want to be, even though you don't yet know where that is....

When you reach the bottom of the steps, you see that there are two doors right ahead of you, one slightly to the right and one slightly to the left. These two doors look different from each other. Allow yourself to stand there and get a feel for these doors. One of them will "pull" you a little more than the other. Allow yourself to get a feel for which door you want to go through....

Now allow yourself to move toward the door you want to go through. Take a look at what the door looks like—its color, what it's made of. Now allow yourself to reach out and grab the handle and open the door. As the door opens, you see some flickering lights coming from the other side.

You step through the doorway and find yourself once again on a landing. This time there are several old stone steps going down, and you see that the flickering lights are coming from lit candles in sconces on the walls. You start walking down these stone steps, feeling more and more relaxed and knowing that where you want to go is just at the bottom of these steps.

As you walk down these steps, you may put your hand out and feel the texture of the wall. You're feeling completely relaxed....You keep walking down these steps until you reach the bottom....

At the bottom of these steps you see straight ahead of you a door—a very old, heavy wooden door. For a handle, it has a big, heavy metal ring. You walk over to this door, knowing that where you want to be is just on the other side of it.

You reach out and grab the metal ring. The door opens toward you. You pull on the metal ring, but the door is so heavy that it hardly moves. So you have to pull even harder, and the door slowly starts to open.

As it opens, you see some beautiful lights. Once the door is open, you step through the doorway—and you now find yourself in the most beautiful room you have ever seen. You stand on the threshold, just looking around this room....

You can't get over how beautiful this room is. It looks like it was designed just for you and for what you love. You see beautifully colored lights. As you stand there taking it all in, you suddenly realize that you feel completely at ease. You just know that this is YOUR room. You allow yourself to stand there a little longer, looking at everything, and you start to walk around, exploring the room....

Then you notice that in the middle of the room there is a long wooden table with several big chairs around it. You realize that you want to go sit down in the chair at the head of the table. So you move toward the table and pull out the chair at the head of the table, and sit down....

As you sit there, you continue to look around the room, marveling at how very at ease you feel here and noticing new details in the room, details you find very pleasing....

You then look over to your right and notice another door in the wall. As you notice this door, you realize that someone or something will be entering the room

through that door—to be with you. You suddenly real-
ize that this visitor is coming to support you and be of
assistance to you. If this feels right to you, you suddenly
feel a pleasant sense of anticipation because you know
that this visitor will be coming here for your benefit.
As you look at the door, it starts to open and you see or
sense someone or a presence entering the room....

Allow yourself to get a sense of the presence enter-
ing the room. Do you see or sense someone (or some-
thing)? Is it male or female—or neuter? Older or
younger? Familiar or not? How is it clothed? Any col-
ors? Does it have a form or just an energy?...

You feel a caring from this presence and realize that
the presence has come here to lend you support. He
or she tells you hello in his or her own way—whether
it's a voice you can hear or a thought formed in your
mind—and then joins you at the table. (Is there a hug,
a handshake?) The presence pulls out a chair and sits
down.

Now the two of you sit there, feeling your presences
merge. You realize that you feel completely comfortable
and at ease—and also more supported....

You look up again and see another door in the wall,
a door that looks different from the other one. As you
see this door, you realize that another presence will
be entering the room to be with you. If this feels right
to you, you wait. As you look at the door, it starts to
open and you see or sense someone or another presence
entering the room....

Allow yourself to get a sense of the presence enter-ing the room. Do you see or sense someone (or some-thing)? Is it male or female—or neuter? Older or younger? Familiar or not? How is it clothed? Any col-ors? Does it have a form or just an energy?...

This presence also greets you in his or her own way and comes over to join you at the table, pulling out a chair and sitting down....

Now the three of you sit there, feeling your pres-ences merge. You're feeling more and more positive and more and more supported....

Once again, you look up and see another door in the wall, which again looks different from the others. You realize that another presence, known or unknown to you, will be entering the room....Then the door opens and you see or sense someone or another pres-ence entering the room....

Allow yourself to get a sense of the presence now entering the room. Do you see or sense someone (or something)? Is it male or female—or neuter? Older or younger? Familiar or not? How is it clothed? Any col-ors? Does it have a form or just an energy?...

This presence also greets you in his or her own way and comes over to join you at the table, pulling out a chair and sitting down....

The four of you now sit there, feeling your presences merge. You're feeling more and more comfortable and have a pleasant sense of anticipation....

Does your group now feel complete? If not, allow yourself to look up and see how many more doors there are in the walls that you hadn't noticed before. As you look at these doors, you realize that you will be joined by more beings coming through these doors to be with you. Allow the doors to open and the beings to enter the room, each greeting you in his or her own fashion, then joining you at the table and sitting down....

Your group now feels complete. You sit there, feeling all of your presences merge....

You now feel them telling you, whether you can hear this as a voice or whether the thought forms in your mind, that they have come here to lend support to you and to counsel and advise you—and that you can ask any question you would like of them. They let you know that they will be happy to answer questions about anything you would like to know....

If this feels right to you, allow yourself to think of questions you would like to ask. As soon as a question forms in your mind, you are given the answer—whether you can "hear" it or not. Sometimes an answer comes from one of them, sometimes from more than one of them. You may hear an answer with your ears, or it may just appear in your mind. In some cases, you may not consciously receive an answer, but you will receive energy from them. If you cannot hear an answer, you're informed that you've been given the answer on a deep level and that it will come to your conscious awareness at a later point and at the right time.

Allow yourself to sit there and ask questions and receive the answers.... (Take as much time for this as necessary.)

After you have asked your last question and have received the answer or energy, you feel them tell you that they have been only too happy to answer your questions and that they would now like to counsel you, perhaps on things you have not asked about. If this feels right to you, allow them to counsel you. Once again, you may feel information coming from one or all of them....

After they finish giving you counsel, they now tell you that they have been only too happy to be here with you and to counsel and advise you—and that you may come back to this room any time you would like, and they and/or others will come here to lend you support as well as counsel.

They are now ready to leave this room, and either one by one or all together they get up, tell you goodbye, perhaps with a hug, and go to their respective doors and leave, closing the doors behind them....

You now find yourself alone in the room again. However, you notice that you don't feel alone. You feel full, fuller than when you came in, and richer in some way. You sit there for a few more minutes looking at all the beautiful things in this special room, which has been designed specifically for you and for your tastes....

Then you realize that you, too, are ready to leave this room. Even though you're about to leave, you know that you can come back here any time you would like. You stand up and walk back to the doorway you entered the room through. When you get there, you turn around and look around this room one more time, perhaps trying to memorize every beautiful detail. You ready yourself to walk through the doorway, knowing that you're not leaving permanently— and that this room will be here waiting for you whenever you wish to return.

You then walk through the doorway and close the door behind you, feeling even fuller. You see the stone steps that you came down and you walk toward them, knowing that you're bringing back with you everything that's important to bring back and leaving the rest behind.

You start back up these steps and find yourself feeling so light that you practically glide up them. You find yourself at the top in no time....

You see the door you walked through, the door you chose. You walk back through it, closing the door behind you. You then see the other steps you came down, and you start back up these, but once again you find yourself gliding to the top....

At the top of these steps, you see the doorway to the hall, and then you see another door to the side. You decide to go through this door to the side instead. You walk over to it and open it. As you do, you find that it leads outside to a beautiful garden in bloom. It's a beautiful sunny day and you walk out into the garden....

You see the flowers and smell their fragrance. You then see a very inviting bench. You walk over to it and sit down, feeling more and more refreshed and real-izing once again that you're bringing back with you everything that's important to bring back and leaving the rest behind. As you sit there, you realize that you're getting ready to come back to the present time....

Whenever you're ready, you can open your eyes and come back to your room and the present time, feeling refreshed and relaxed....

———

How did that go for you? Were you able to get into the meditation well? If you were, allow yourself to notice how you're feeling now. Meditating usually gets us into our center, and we often feel more centered after meditating than we usually do at other times in our lives. Concerns and stress often feel more distant after meditating.

If this is the first time that you've meditated, make a mental note of how you feel now, or make a journal entry to refer back to in the future. The more frequently you meditate and get into your center, the more you'll be able to retain this feeling, or at least some part of it, at other times in your life.

If you feel that you weren't able to get into the meditation, or if it was difficult for you, please come back to it at a later time. You might wait a week and try it again. For the purpose of learning how to tune in and optimize your ability to access intuitive information, it's important to be able to get into that meditative state. Just wait a week or two and try the meditation again, until you feel that you've been able to get into it.

If you were able to get into the meditation and find yourself "in your center," make a mental note of how this feels. This is not only good for stress relief, but it can also help you with any boundary issues. If you remember how it feels to be in your center, you'll also notice more easily when you're pulled out of your center. This is one of the first steps toward being able to erect boundaries when necessary. So allow yourself to notice and remember how this feels, if you were able to get into the meditation and get to a deeper level of consciousness.

Were you able to get any intuitive information or insights? If you did, allow yourself to make a note of how the information came to you (which form or forms) and how it felt. For example, were you able to see images or hear sounds? Even if you feel that you didn't get any information, the important thing is having been able to get into the meditation itself and that deeper level of consciousness. If you were able to get information, allow yourself to make a note of it, both mentally and in your journal. You'll want to review your journal from time to time because some information may make more sense to you down the road.

If the information you received wasn't literal, make a note of it anyway. In the next chapter, we'll be going over how to interpret symbolic and figurative information. The appendix on dreams also goes over some points on interpreting information.

You may also find yourself receiving even more information, as well as clarification on some of what you got, in the next several days as you go about your business. Often a meditation or even tuning in isn't really over when you stop doing it at the time. It can continue to reverberate and produce more information and realizations. This is one wonderful aspect of both your intuition and deeper levels of consciousness.

Exercise: Shorter Guided Meditation

While you're learning how to receive intuitive information on demand, it can be useful to be able to quickly get into a deeper level of consciousness, so you can quickly reach the state of mind where you can access your intuition. This is what you'll need to be able to do in order to tune in to get information. This Shorter Guided Meditation will give you more practice with that. However, if you had trouble getting into the longer initial meditation, I recommend doing that one a few more times until you've been successful at getting into it *before* trying this next one.

> *Allow yourself to get very comfortable, whether sitting or lying down. Take some deep breaths, allowing yourself to release any concerns or worries—anything you've had on your mind. Simply allow yourself to relax as you continue to take some deep breaths….*
>
> *Now allow yourself to imagine a place that would be perfect for you. This could a place you've been to or a place you've never been to. It could be a real place or an imaginary place. It doesn't matter which it is or where it is as long as it feels like it would be perfect for you.*

Allow yourself to get a full sense of this place—what it looks like, feels like, sounds like, smells like....

Now imagine yourself in this place. As you now find yourself in this place, allow yourself to get a sense of how comfortable you feel here. Allow yourself to realize that this is YOUR place—a place where you can be comfortable, where you can feel completely at ease and powerful....

Allow yourself now to walk around this place, touching things, feeling the temperature—and feeling more and more at home....

Allow yourself to realize that this is uniquely your place and that nothing can affect you here, unless you want it to. Take some time to fully explore this place and enjoy yourself....

When you're ready, open your eyes and come back to the present, feeling fully refreshed and energized. Notice how you feel and how this differs from how you felt before you did this exercise.

———

Were you able to get into that meditation? Did you notice that you felt differently afterward? Hopefully you felt more centered. Sometimes being in a wonderful place can be very calming and centering. If you experienced that sort of effect, you may want to make a mental note of what this place was like, so you can return to it in the future for other exercises, as need be. Feeling yourself in a positive, calming, and comfortable place can be useful at times in accessing information, and you can create your own exercises in which you go to a place like this in order to access information.

Exercise: Guided Meditation to Get a Sense of Your Intuition

Have you ever thought about what your own intuition is like—what it looks or feels like? You may feel more comfortable exploring your intuition if you have a better feel for it and its attributes. In other words, personalizing and "befriending" your intuition could make it even easier for you to work with it and receive information.

The next exercise is another guided meditation that can lead you to better know what your intuition is like and what it may feel or look like.

Allow yourself to get very comfortable, whether sitting or lying down. As you get more comfortable physically, allow yourself to take some deep breaths and begin to relax, feeling the various parts of your body easily letting go and relaxing. Continue to take some deep breaths as you prepare to go on a journey that will help you uncover and use your intuition, trusting that what you experience will be exactly what you need to experience....

Continue to take some deep breaths as you feel the different parts of your body letting go and relaxing, and as you sink more and more into the chair, floor, etc., that your body is resting on....

Now find a comfortable breathing pattern, and allow yourself to see or feel yourself walking around a beautiful place, a place that feels completely comfortable to you. You may be inside or outside, walking through a forest or field or even floating through the air. Just allow yourself to move around this wonderful place you find yourself in....

Allow yourself to smell any ambient odors, feel what the temperature is like, notice any sounds....

As you continue to explore this place, noticing how comfortable you feel here, you find yourself lightly contemplating your intuition and wishing you could know more about it, how it expresses itself to you and how it works. This is just a thought you have, and you don't feel any intensity attached to it—just a light thought, because you're thoroughly enjoying being in this place and exploring it....

You hear or see some movement over to the side, and all of a sudden a very young child appears. The child smiles at you in a very loving way and skips over to you....

Looking up at you, the child says, "I'm so happy to see you! I haven't seen you in so long!" As the child tells you this, you find yourself hearing a voice either through your ears or as a thought in your mind. Either way is fine....

You find yourself quite touched by this child, and you find yourself smiling back. The child takes you by the hand and says to you, "I'm so happy to see you again! I really want to show you something. I know you'll want to see it. Please let me show you!"

If this feels right to you, allow the child to lead you by the hand, noticing where the child leads you and the scenery along the way. You find yourself knowing on a deep level that the child does indeed have something important to show you....

The child leads you to a room that's full of display cases and says, "What I want to show you is in here. I know you'll really like it! Please close your eyes—I'll tell you when you can open them."

As the child leads you past the display cases, the child says, "That's the one! That's the one I want to show you!" The two of you stop walking, and the child says, "In this display case is your intuition and everything about it—how it feels and how it works."

You begin to feel a pleasant sense of anticipation, and then the child says, "Open your eyes now and see what's in here for you."

You allow yourself to open your eyes and look in the case, taking in everything that's in there. You can see, sense, feel, and hear. Allow yourself to get a full sense of everything in the display case....

The child then says, "Isn't that wonderful? It's just perfect!" The child then begins to remind you of times in the past when your intuition spoke to you and when you were able to get intuitive information. You allow yourself to listen to the child and fully remember each experience and how it felt....

The child then says, "I'm so glad you let me show you all of this! I could show you a lot more, but I'll save some for another time, because I'll be here any time you want me to."

The child gives you a hug and then skips off and leaves.

Allow yourself to savor this experience, knowing that you'll bring back all the important information and leave the rest behind. Allow yourself to feel grateful for the experience and for this wonderful little child....

You realize that you're now ready to leave this place and come back to the present, knowing once again that you'll bring back everything important for you to bring back and leave the rest behind—and that you'll come back refreshed and relaxed....

Whenever you're ready, come back to the present, feeling refreshed and energized and knowing that something has shifted inside you in a positive way....

———

I hope that you were able to get some good information through this exercise. Allow yourself to make some notes about what you experienced and saw and felt, as well as how your intuition appeared. Make some notes in your journal as well as mentally.

Did everything you experienced or saw make sense to you? If not, you can always ask for clarification or more information through tuning in or through seeing what else comes to you in the next few days or weeks. Remember that these exercises will often continue to reverberate—or continue working—after you've finished them, especially those that move energy. An exercise like this can be the gift that keeps on giving.

Did everything about your intuition make sense to you? Did you see aspects of your intuition that you were already familiar with—or did anything surprise you about your intuition? If so, what does that tell you? Can you recognize aspects of your intuition that were present in any of your prior experiences with it? Are there any implications in what you saw or experienced in this exercise for how you can work with your intuition or new things that you can do with it?

Did you find yourself in a different location from the one in the Shorter Guided Meditation (in chapter 5), or a similar one? Either way, allow yourself to make a note of where you were. There may be times when you'll primarily find yourself in the same place. If that's the case, however, please don't close yourself off to the possibility of going to new places. Wherever you find yourself going in an exercise is usually where you need to go, and where you'll be able to get the most out of the experience. The most important thing is that this be a place where you feel comfortable, calm, secure, and able to access information, irrespective of where it is or what it looks like.

I feel that the meditative exercises in this chapter are necessary to do to enable you to get to that deeper level of consciousness where it is easier to access intuitive information, if that is something you haven't done before. By now, you should be able to get into a deeper meditative state of consciousness. *If you haven't been able to do that, please do these exercises over again before going on to the next ones.*

If you were able to get into those deeper levels of consciousness fairly easily, you should be ready to move on to the next exercises. Once again, the method I teach and that I'm sharing with you is that of tuning in, in which you quickly go to a deeper level of consciousness (that is not quite as deep as meditation) in order to receive intuitive information quickly and easily, while also bypassing any of your personal stuff to the greatest degree possible. The previous exercises should have enabled you to do that. In the next exercises, you will apply that practice to specific questions or issues.

six

Beginner Exercises to Develop Your Intuition

Now that you've practiced getting into an intuitive state of consciousness through meditation, we'll start doing some intuitive exercises. These exercises will enable you to begin developing your intuition and will draw upon different intuitive skills and forms.

You may find all of the exercises equally easy, or you may find that you're better at some than others. If the latter proves to be true, that would probably indicate that you have a more natural orientation toward the type(s) or form(s) of intuition that the exercises you find easier to do represent. If you find yourself better at one particular form (seeing images, for example) than others (psychometry, or touching objects, for example), that doesn't mean your ability with other forms won't strengthen over time. While I tend to kinesthetically feel energy and get impressions, I consistently find that I also get visual images, feelings, and other forms at times. Don't tell yourself that you can only experience intuition in certain ways, because you'll be limiting yourself and closing the door on other ways. You should find yourself pleasantly surprised over time by what you can experience and access—as long as you remain open to the possibilities.

I've included a variety of exercises to allow you to experience a wide range of possible ways to receive intuitive information. One beauty of intuition is that we can design many different types of exercises in order to access information. The exercises you'll see in this chapter and the next do not represent the full range of possibilities. You'll be able to come up with some of your own over time.

You can be alone while doing most of these exercises. There are some, however, that require someone else to be present, so please keep this in mind so you can plan on finding someone to do them with.

It will be helpful for you to make notes in your journal of what you experience with these exercises and review your notes from time to time in the future.

You'll want to review the instructions and things to keep in mind that I shared at the beginning of chapter 5 before doing these exercises, just as a reminder.

Exercise: Receiving an Answer to a Question through Imagery

Often when we're working with our intuition, we're looking for information about specific issues or questions. So let's start working on that.

For this exercise, allow yourself to think of something you'd like to get some information on, perhaps a question you've had or an issue you've been focusing on. Make sure this is an open-ended question rather than a yes/no question. Once you have your topic or question in mind, you can start on the exercise.

Close your eyes and get very comfortable. Take some deep breaths, allowing yourself to easily relax and get into a pleasant place....

With your question in mind, imagine or feel that you're walking down a road looking for information on your question. You come to a quaint town, one that's obviously a few centuries old. Allow yourself to walk around this town....You then find yourself in the town square looking at all the old, somewhat imposing buildings. You see a court house and a hall of records. Then you see a library with large columns at the front of the building and a set of stairs leading gracefully to the entrance.

Allow yourself to walk up these steps and enter the library....

Inside you see a huge collection of books arranged neatly on numerous bookshelves. There's a pleasant, calm feeling here, with lovely light filtering down through the windows. Allow yourself to walk around the library, feeling the temperature, listening to any sounds, etc., until you find a row of books that appeals to you....

Standing in front of this row, allow yourself to see which book pulls you or appeals to you. (You won't need to read the titles. It will be the feel of the book that pulls you to it.) Once you find it, allow yourself to pick it up from the shelf. It's quite heavy, as it's an old and over-sized book....

Carrying the book with you, find the nearest table and walk over and lay the book on it. Hold your question lightly in mind, take a deep breath, and then allow yourself to open the book to any page....

Once you have the book open, see what is on the page, whether text or pictures—or anything else. Allow yourself to get a full sense of the contents on the opened page or pages....

If you'd like more information, you can open the book to another random page and see what is on that one....

Now pick up the book and carefully place it back on the shelf as you hold the information from the book in mind....

You may now leave the library and prepare to come back to the present time, bringing back with you any information that's important for you to bring back and leaving the rest behind.

When you're ready, open your eyes and come back to the present time, feeling refreshed and fuller.

———

After finishing the exercise, you'll want to think about and review the information you received. As you probably noticed, the way in which you accessed information in this exercise was indirect, through reading random pages, rather than direct, through asking specifically about the topic. Nevertheless, the information you received should be helpful and appropriate. Make a note of the information that was there for you, and write some notes in your journal.

Was the information you received literal, or do you need more information or clarification? If you need clarification, you can simply tune in and ask for it. If you received information that's symbolic, you may need to work at determining what the symbols mean. You can do this by free-associating or by asking yourself what the symbol means to you; for example, "When I think of a mountain, I think of _____" or "A mountain is _____."

Do you feel that you got all the information you needed on the issue? If not, you can always repeat the exercise and get more information.

The point is that there are things you can do with the information after having received it. We can usually do more with information we've received, and we'll be delving into this more later on in chapter 7.

For now, remember these two important points:

1. If you're not sure what the information was telling you, you can always ask for clarification or tune in for more information.

2. If you received any symbolic information, you can always free-associate to determine the meanings or ask yourself, "What does this thing mean to me?"

If you feel that you've received the information you needed, allow yourself to notice how you feel. Often when we've gotten information we were looking for or that answered a question we had, we feel better. We may feel lighter or clearer or fuller. If you allow yourself to identify how you feel when you've gotten answers you felt you needed, you can be on the lookout for that feeling in the future, to use as an indication of whether you've accessed what you needed to get. You might want to make a note in your journal of how you felt, to have for future reference. Of course, you may feel better in a different way than you do now, and that's fine.

There may be times when we need to do additional things with the information we've received, as I mentioned, and we'll be learning about this in the next chapter.

This exercise was one in which we used an indirect method with imagery to access information on a topic of interest to us. In the next exercise, you'll experience a more direct way of accessing the information you're looking for, by directly tuning in.

Exercise: Getting an Answer to a Question by Simply Tuning In

You've now been able to go to deeper levels of consciousness through guided meditation, and you've experienced receiving information on a subject you wanted information about through the means of imagery in a deeper state of consciousness. Using imagery can be an easier way to access information, but you also want to be able to receive information directly without any crutches. So the next step is to be direct and tune in to receive information. This is what you'd like to be able to do on demand, so you can receive information on topics at will and quickly. You'll remember that in chapter 4 we went over the procedure for tuning in. If you need to review that procedure, you can do that now.

To prepare for this next step, think of another question or topic you'd like to have some information about, preferably an open-ended question rather than a yes/no one. This should be a different topic or question from any of the previous ones you've used. Have your question in mind as you practice tuning in.

Get comfortable physically and close your eyes. Start taking some deep breaths until you feel yourself relaxing....

Keep breathing a little more deeply than normal while you clear your mind, relaxing more and more....

Now pose the question you have and release it from your mind. Wait, making sure to keep your mind clear of your normal mind chatter, so you can see what comes to you. Observe what comes into your mind, no matter what it is, as well as how you feel, including in your body. (How does the information present itself to you and in what form[s]?) If the information feels like it's your normal internal mental chatter, release it from your mind, take some more deep breaths, and clear your mind again...waiting to see what comes to you.

If you feel yourself getting distracted or starting to heed what is going on outside of you (noises, other distractions, etc.), start the process over again. Make sure

you don't rush this. Allow yourself to wait patiently for
information to come to you and to form in your mind
or register in your body.

———

Did that go well for you, and were you able to receive some information? If so, how did you experience the information? How did it come to you and speak to you and in which form(s)? Was the information subtle or blatant? Was it literal or straightforward, or symbolic? If you were able to get some information, acknowledge that you were successful at this. If you found it difficult, you can always repeat this exercise later on and try it on a regular basis.

Doing these exercises with a friend or in a class or workshop rather than alone will enable you to learn how other people are experiencing their intuition, which can be instructive and helpful for you. I've seen over and over again through my teaching that students often learn as much from what others are experiencing and sharing as from their own experiences. If you can do this exercise with other people present, encourage others to share their experiences and discuss them. There could be some wonderful synergy as a result!

Remember to practice tuning in on a regular basis. Being able to tune in and quickly access intuitive information is a skill that will improve over time, with regular practice. The more you practice tuning in, the easier you should find it and the more successful you should be in accessing information, as long as you don't overdo it by either obsessing about it or working on it all the time. Your intuitive skills should grow with regular, but not necessarily daily, practice.

Exercise: Simulation of Remote Viewing

Now that you've experienced tuning in and you've been successful at receiving information, we'll practice working with some specific forms of intuition. The first one we'll practice is the visual form—receiving visual images or focusing on visual targets.

This next exercise is one that approximates remote viewing. You may have heard that the U.S. government had a secret program using a form of ESP. That form of ESP was remote viewing. It was a program in which people were trained to get information clairvoyantly on military or other politically significant targets that were located at a distance. While this program used to be top secret, several of the former participants (called "remote viewers") have since come forward and written or spoken about the program.

This exercise is a rough simulation of remote viewing. When I use this exercise in workshops or classes, I use photographs and pictures from magazines that I place in envelopes, which participants use as targets. This procedure has some built-in limitations and isn't fail-safe, because participants could be telepathically picking up on my unconscious memory of photos rather than intuitively honing in on the photos themselves. Obviously we can't follow that same exact procedure here, but we can use another one.

In lieu of my providing you with an envelope containing a target photo, you'll use a magazine that you *have not* read or looked through. It's critical that you haven't looked through the contents.

What you'll be aiming at with this exercise is seeing what information comes to you visually or in any other form. Remember that the goal of this exercise *is not to guess what the picture is of.* You'll want, instead, to see what comes to you and in what forms as you use a page in the magazine as a focal point.

> *Choose a magazine or book with pictures that you have neither read nor opened. Once you have chosen the magazine or book, think of a page number in the publication and write that page number down. Now place the publication on a surface, whether the floor, a table, etc., in front of where you will sit, with it still closed.*
>
> *Now sit or lie down facing the closed magazine or book, and get comfortable physically. Close your eyes, take some deep breaths, and get completely relaxed. Allow yourself to focus on the page number, and then release it from your mind....*
>
> *Wait...and see what comes into your mind and consciousness. See what appears and in what form, as well as how you feel, both emotionally and in your body....*
>
> *If you get distracted, clear your mind and take some deep breaths—and start over. Allow yourself to see what comes into your consciousness and how it presents itself, including how your body feels....*

When you feel that you've received all the information you can, open your eyes and come back to the room you're in.

———

Okay, don't open the magazine yet. First, allow yourself to review everything that came to you during the exercise. Make a note in your journal of both the information itself and the form(s) in which it came to you. After you've done that, open the magazine to the page number you had focused on. Is there a photo on that page? If not, look at the page before and the page after or another page until you find one with a photo on it.

Once you're on a page with a photo, take a look at everything in the photo and try to get a sense of what in the photo was triggering what you were getting. It could be a color, a curve or shape, a feeling the picture projects, feelings conveyed by any people in the photo, and so forth. There should be elements in the photo that you were picking up on and that triggered the information you received. As you note each one, allow yourself to realize how particular, even minute, details can give us information. This should give you even more validation of your intuitive ability and allow you to see how it might work for you. It's less important to intuitively "see" the entire picture and figure out what the picture was than to accurately receive information on its components and elements.

If you'd like more practice with this type of exercise, you can always do it more times with other pages in the same or a different magazine, and you will likely see your ability improve each time.

Exercise: Psychometry

Next we'll practice psychometry. Do you remember that one form of intuition is that of touch, that some people can touch objects and receive information or get impressions from them? This is called psychometry, and people who tend to be tactile will often be sensitive to objects and more easily receive information from touching them. As I shared earlier, some psychics who work with police departments to help solve crimes may practice psychometry and may be called upon to hold an object belonging to a missing person or victim of a crime in order to get information about the missing person's whereabouts or about the perpetrator of the crime.

You may be naturally adept at psychometry, or, if not, you should see your ability with it improve with practice. For this exercise, you will ideally be reading an object belonging to someone you don't know well. There are many situations in which we come into contact with people we don't know very well, so allow yourself to think of someone you can ask to participate in this exercise. After you've thought of someone, obtain an object belonging to him or her and hold it in your hand. You'll need the person to be either present or available by phone to share the impressions you get.

Close your eyes and take some deep breaths, relaxing and getting into a deeper level of consciousness. Allow

*yourself to become very relaxed....Remind yourself of
the object you're holding and then release any thought
of it. With a clear mind, allow yourself to see what
comes to your awareness—any thoughts, images, feelings or emotions, etc. Also note any changes or feelings
in your body. If nothing comes in, clear your mind,
taking more deep breaths if you need to. Then remind
yourself again of the object you're holding and how it
feels in your hand. Release any thought of it again and
wait to see what comes in....*

*As you receive information and impressions, describe
them to the person who owns the object, asking about the
relevance of what you're getting. Once you've received all
the information you can get, open your eyes.*

————

Were you able to receive some impressions and information? Were you able to validate the information you
got with the person who owns the object? Being able to
receive confirmation of what you get is very important in
developing your intuition. It will give you more confidence
and instruct you about some of the workings of your own
intuition. You'll want to make a note in your journal of the
information you received and the feedback from the other
person, as well as any new insights about your intuition.

You may find that the owner of the object wants you to
get more information or details about the object, expanding
on what you've already gotten. If this is the case, just tune in
again and see what else you get.

You can do this exercise additional times with other objects belonging to other people, which should enable you to improve upon your ability with psychometry. This will give you yet another tool in your toolbox of intuitive abilities and skills.

Exercise: Decision-Making through Experience and Feeling

There are many different ways to receive intuitive information. This is a wonderful aspect of intuition, as it gives you more resources to draw upon with your own intuition. This exercise allows you to receive information to aid in the decision-making process when faced with different possible options.

Trying to choose among different options can be quite frustrating at times. We may mentally go over and over the potential benefits and downsides of all the options, leading us to feel confused and mentally burned out. When faced with several alternatives, we can get to the point where we can't see the forest for the trees.

Intuition can allow us to cut through the confusion and frustration and see things and factors that can lead us to know which is the best option, along with what the true benefits and outcomes will be.

In order to do this exercise, allow yourself to think of a decision you're trying to make that involves a choice among at least three different options.

Begin by sitting or lying down and getting very comfortable. Close your eyes and begin to take some deep breaths, relaxing more and more with each breath. As you breathe deeply, allow yourself to release any tension or soreness, relaxing deeply....

As you find yourself more relaxed, allow yourself to see or feel yourself walking down a road. You're in no rush to get anywhere. You just simply walk along—and, as you do, allow yourself to hold lightly in mind the decision you're trying to make and the options you're considering. As you walk along, allow yourself to notice the scenery and what you find around you....

As you walk along, you find yourself at a fork in the road. In fact, there are as many forks as options you're considering. Allow yourself to note these forks and then approach one of them. This first fork will represent one of your options. Allow yourself to walk down this fork, fully noticing and experiencing what or whom you encounter along the way. Pay attention to how you feel as you do this. Keep walking down this fork until you feel that you have experienced everything there is for you there....

Once you have experienced everything down this fork, turn around and walk back the way you came until you reach the main road....

When you reach the main road, allow yourself to approach another fork, knowing that it represents yet another of your options. Allow yourself to walk down this fork, exploring it and experiencing everything and everyone there, while paying attention to how you feel....

Once you have experienced everything down this fork, once again turn around and walk back to the main road. Continue to explore each fork in the same manner until you have walked down and explored all the forks, representing each of your options....

Once you have finished exploring these forks and have returned to the main road, allow yourself to walk back down the main road the way you came. As you do, allow yourself to mull over the information you gained by exploring the different forks and options. You once again begin to notice the landscape and surroundings, noticing how you now feel....

As you continue to walk back down the main road, you notice that you're feeling better and better, clearer and more refreshed. Allow yourself to continue walking until you feel ready to come back to this room. When you feel ready, open your eyes and find yourself feeling refreshed and renewed.

———

Were you able to feel or sense which option was the best one for you? Did anything you experienced during this exercise and down any of the forks surprise you? Often when people do an exercise like this, they will encounter things they had not anticipated or taken into consideration that could affect the decision they make, which is another reason that this can be such a useful exercise to do. Once again, it highlights the fact that there are numerous ways in which you can get needed intuitive information for yourself.

Using our intuition in this way allows us to bypass our left brain. It's often true that when we're trying to make a decision involving different factors and options, we will consider all factors and options, using our logic to analyze and weigh them. This is not to say that we shouldn't use our logic. However, this rational process doesn't allow us to consider or take into account unforeseen factors, and, as already mentioned, it can also lead us to feel overwhelmed or burned out. Using our intuition in an exercise like this not only allows us to bypass our logical left brain when it would be helpful for us to do so; it also allows us to perceive and sense things we had not considered, giving us even more information with which to make our decision.

This is not the only exercise that can help you with decision-making. In time, you may find or create additional exercises to use when you're similarly needing to make a decision with several possible options.

The next exercise represents yet another way in which you can intuitively get a sense of what to do when faced with a decision.

Exercise: Decision-Making through Body Wisdom

You'll want to prepare for this exercise by thinking of a decision you're trying to make—a different one from the last exercise—for which you're considering different options. You'll want to have those options in mind as you do this exercise, which will represent yet another way of getting information about a potential decision with different options.

Sit or lie down and get very comfortable. Close your eyes and begin to take some deep breaths, relaxing more and more with each breath. As you breathe deeply, allow yourself to release any tension or soreness, relaxing deeply....

As you relax, hold lightly in mind the decision you're trying to make. Now allow yourself to remember the beautiful place you identified previously in either the Shorter Guided Meditation or the Guided Meditation to Get a Sense of Your Intuition in chapter 5. As you call that place to mind, you now feel yourself there. If you want to walk around and explore this place again, you can do so. If you find yourself in a different beautiful place, that's fine. Allow yourself to walk around and explore whatever place you're in. Feel the temperature here, and note any sounds or smells....

Now call to mind one course of action you're considering taking.... Then clear that from your mind.

Allow yourself to imagine that you have taken that course of action, and now see how you feel, including how your body feels....

Once you have gotten a sense of how you feel after having taken that particular course of action, clear your mind again....

Still feeling yourself in this beautiful and comfortable place, allow yourself to call to mind another course of action you're considering. Once you have it in mind, see how you feel, including how your body feels.... Now clear your mind again.

Once again, allow yourself to imagine that you have now taken the course of action you're considering. See how you now feel, including in your body....

Allow yourself to continue to do this for each course of action you're contemplating, making sure to clear your mind in between....

Once you have imagined each course of action, allow yourself to be in that beautiful place again, soaking in the positive feel and energy of the place. Know that you're getting ready to come back to the room you're sitting or lying in and that you'll feel refreshed and relaxed.

Whenever you're ready, open your eyes and come back to your room.

———

Did you feel different things in your body for each option? If you were successful at feeling different things in your body as a response to the various options you were considering, make a note of them. Do these different responses help you in knowing which option(s) would be better for you? Be sure to make some journal entries about what you're taking away from this exercise.

As you've experienced through this exercise, your body can be an aid to you in making decisions. It will register responses and give you information about possibilities that you have not yet tried or considered. Never discount your body's wisdom and awareness of your needs and preferences.

I have used this exercise with some of my private clients when I've sensed that a part of them knew which course of action would be best for them, and I've yet to find a person who didn't get useful information from his or her body.

Remember to enlist your body's assistance at times in making decisions.

Exercise: When Faced with a Yes/No Question

The next exercise is a rather simple one and one that you can use whenever you have one of those frequent questions that can be answered "yes" or "no."

Think of a question you have that can only be answered with a yes or no. Keep that question in mind as you do this exercise.

Close your eyes and take some deep breaths, relaxing and getting into a deeper level of consciousness. Allow yourself to get very relaxed, and feel your body sinking into the surface you're sitting or lying on….

Lightly hold your question in mind and then release it….

Now allow yourself to see a table close to you, whether in front of you or over to the side. You see a couple of pieces of paper lying on the table. Allow yourself to look more closely at those two sheets of paper. On one, you see the word "yes" written. Allow yourself to look at it a while longer….

On the other sheet of paper, you see the word "no" written. You look at that a while longer….

Clear that out of your mind. Now pose your question once again. With your question in mind, allow yourself to look at the sheet of paper with the "yes" on it. What does the "yes" look like now?...

Clear your mind. Now pose your question one more time. With your question in mind, allow yourself to look at the other sheet of paper with the "no" on it. What does the "no" look like now?...

Clear that out of your mind. Focus on your question another time. Then look at the sheet of paper with the "yes" on it. The word "yes" lifts off the paper and approaches you. Then it just enters your body. After it does, allow yourself to see how it feels in your body....

Clear your mind once again. The paper is now gone from your body. Then focus on your question one more time. Look at the sheet of paper with the "no" on it. As you look at it, the word "no" lifts off the paper and approaches you. Then it just enters your body. After it does, allow yourself to see how it feels in your body....

Allow yourself to get a sense of how each word felt—and also what that tells you about your question.

Once you've gotten a sense of this, allow yourself to open your eyes.

————

Did you get an answer to your question with this exercise? Did you find the words on the paper looking different from each other both before and after you asked your question? What happened after the sheets of paper entered your body? Did your body feel different? If so, did that give you some information? Make some notes in your journal about what you experienced and any insights you gained into your intuition.

This exercise shows you that you can get a yes/no answer either through imagery (with the sheet of paper) or through your body. You can also adapt this exercise and just focus on getting an answer through your body. Another variation would be to create a scenario with someone in it whom you consider to be very wise, whether you know the person or not, and pose the question to him or her.

Exercise: Imagery to Strengthen Your Intuition

Next we'll work on strengthening our intuition and our confidence with it through imagery. One thing that can stand in the way of improving our ability to work with intuition is a lack of confidence. If we doubt that we're intuitive or if we doubt that we can be very successful in receiving intuitive information on a regular basis, we can be helping to create a self-fulfilling prophecy, hindering our intuitive ability.

This exercise will help build your confidence in your intuition in an unusual way.

Sit or lie down and get very comfortable. Close your eyes and begin to take some deep breaths, relaxing more and more with each breath. As you breathe deeply, allow yourself to release any tension or soreness, relaxing deeply....

As you find yourself relaxed, find a comfortable breathing pattern that's a little deeper than normal, but not so deep that it's labored....

Now allow yourself to see or feel yourself walking through a lovely place. You may be inside or outside, wherever you find yourself walking. You note how lovely this place is and how comfortable you feel here. You note everything around you—what things look like, what the temperature feels like, any sounds here, any fragrances....

As you walk along, you find yourself thinking about your intuition and your desire to strengthen it. As you do this, someone comes to mind whom you admire for his or her intuitive ability and integrity in using it. This could be a person you know personally or someone you know of. It could even be a group of people, as long as they're adept at using their intuition. We'll refer to this person or group as a master. You may feel that you'd like to be able to know how he or she—or even they—work with intuition, so that you can learn from this expert.

As you walk along, you see the master right ahead of you. The master smiles at you. Allow yourself to walk over and approach this expert....

The two of you hug and begin to walk together. You feel great warmth coming from him or her to you and you convey how much you admire the master's intuitive ability and integrity, adding that you would love to hone your ability and learn from what can be conveyed. The master smiles in response and lets you know that he or she would be happy to help in any way and that you may ask any questions. If this feels right to you, allow yourself to ask this master questions about intuition in general, your intuition, and how his or her intuition works....

After you have asked your last question, the master describes to you how he or she receives information and what it feels like. You listen and make mental notes....

After this, the master asks if you would like to actually experience how he or she experiences intuition. You can do this by merging with him or her, or the master can project to you the energy of receiving information. If this feels right to you, allow yourself to choose which method you would prefer and let the master know your choice. You can now merge with the master, with your consciousness entering the master's body, or your own body entering it—or allow the master to project the energy of receiving intuitive information to you....

The master now starts to work with his or her intuition, accessing information. As he or she does this, you are now able to actually experience and feel what this master experiences. Allow yourself to fully experience this for as long as you need to....

Once you have experienced as much as you need to, you disengage and separate from the master, if you have merged, or you disengage from the energy projected to you. You thank the master for this experience and for answering your questions. The master graciously lets you know that he or she is only too happy to do so. You express your gratitude again, and the master leaves. You now continue walking in another direction….

As you walk along, you mull over what you have experienced, knowing that you're richer and fuller for this experience. You find a comfortable place to sit down, continuing to mull over your experience….

You are now ready to open your eyes and come back to your room, bringing back everything that's helpful for you to bring back and leaving the rest behind, and knowing that when you do, you'll feel refreshed and relaxed. Whenever you're ready, open your eyes and come back to your room.

———

How did that exercise go for you? Were you able to get information from the other person or group? Were you successful in feeling or experiencing some of what the person felt while accessing his or her intuition? Allow yourself to make notes in your journal about any of the information you received and what you experienced.

This is admittedly a more unusual exercise. However, it draws upon the fact that there is a wide range of information available to us, as well as a wealth of unanticipated resources. Furthermore, learning how others experience intuition can further your progress with your own. I've seen this over and over again in my workshops and classes on intuition. As I mentioned, students will often learn as much from what others are experiencing as from their own experiences or my guidance and instruction.

As with many of the other exercises, you may find more information coming to you afterward. If you do, fine. And if you don't, that's also fine.

You can also revisit this exercise from time to time. I recommend not doing it too often, though, as that could lessen what you get out of it. Doing it a few times a year would be optimum, although if you encounter someone new whose ability you really respect, go ahead and try it.

Exercise: Practice in Reading Someone Else

If you want to develop your intuition to the point where you're working professionally with others, you'll need to become proficient at reading other people. Even if you don't plan on becoming a professional with your intuition, being able to intuitively read other people can be helpful in your relationships, as you'll gain more insight into the people in your life. A lot of conflict in relationships comes from misunderstandings and misjudging another's position or motivation. So honing your ability to read others can be hugely beneficial for you in your life.

For this exercise, you'll need to identify someone to read. Ideally this will be someone you're not in close relationship to and don't know well. Additionally, you may feel more comfortable having the other person physically there with you, as opposed to trying to read him or her at a distance. As you gain proficiency with your intuition and develop your ability to sense and read energy, you will be able to read people at a distance. Most of the consultations I do are by telephone, and I've never needed someone to be present in order to read him or her. Remember that energy is non-local, as is information, so you should be able to read a person's energy and receive information for and about him or her at a distance as you gain more experience with this over time. However, we'll start out with the person you're reading being in proximity to you, in the same room.

When you ask the person if he or she will participate in this exercise, also ask for permission to read him or her. You should always ask permission to read someone directly. Let the person know that whatever transpires in this exercise and any information gained will be held in strict confidence. Confidentiality should always be maintained when you get information for or about someone else.

Once you have the person there with you, make sure you're sitting fairly close to each other, preferably within a few feet of each other. You'll also want to turn off any phones, the television, etc., to ensure that you're not interrupted or distracted during the exercise.

Sitting with this person, allow yourself to close your eyes and take some deep breaths, relaxing more and more and sinking into a deeper level of consciousness. Allow yourself to be completely centered and relaxed….

Now allow yourself to shift your awareness—still with your eyes closed—to the other person. Try to get a sense of what the other person's energy feels like. Don't work too hard at this. Merely allow yourself to feel the other person's energy. Is it smooth, pointy or jagged, light, heavy, pleasant, swirling or moving, stationary, etc.?…

Now try to get a sense of what the other person is like on the inside—not how the person presents him- or herself, but who the real person is deep down. What are his or her true attributes and characteristics? Who is the real person? You can verbalize what you're getting and ask for feedback or confirmation. After you've felt the other person's energy, allow yourself to simply see what comes into your awareness, running what you receive by the other person....

Ask the other person if he or she has anything he or she would like for you to look at and receive information on. If so, allow yourself to pose each question the person has, using the tuning-in procedure, and then see what comes into your awareness and in what form. Remember to clear your mind each time after you pose a question and then simply observe what comes to you, including how your body feels. As you receive information, allow yourself to mention it to the other person, continuing to receive feedback and confirmation....

When you feel that you have gotten as much information as you can, open your eyes and come back to the room you're in.

————

How did this one go? Were you able to get some information—and confirmation of what you received? Did anything you got surprise you?

You can also look for more confirmation from the other person after ending the exercise. Even if the person doesn't agree with what you got or isn't sure of it, you can always tune back in to verify what you received or seek more information and/or another way to express and convey the information. Just because someone doesn't quite grasp what you've conveyed doesn't mean that you can't dialogue with him or her to achieve better understanding. I frequently encounter a need with clients to rephrase or get additional information to ensure that my client understands the information and is on the same page. (This may be especially true for me, as some of my information comes in the form of impressions and appears in a very abstract way. I frequently feel that I have to "step it down" in order to get the information to a level where it can be put into words.)

Don't be discouraged if this exercise felt difficult to do. Your ability will improve just by your continuing to work at it, even if you're feeling your way along with it at times. I was feeling my way along initially and found my abilities getting much stronger with practice over time.

I encourage you to do this exercise several times, with different people. Everyone is different, and you should see yourself getting different information from one person to the next, because people are true individuals. I still get information I've never gotten before when I read a person's essence, in terms of how a person's energy works and the type of energy. If you find yourself getting information you've never gotten before, you're more likely to be getting true and reliable intuitive information, rather than putting other people into preconceived categories.

You should find your confidence improving over time as you read more people. Don't worry if you initially feel a little self-conscious or timid, as that should diminish over time with more practice and positive feedback—and as you see your ability growing.

Remember to maintain confidentiality at all times. This is the same code of ethics as with doctors, therapists, etc. When people have readings done, they expect that the practitioner is a professional and will not share personal information with other people.

These are the beginner exercises. I hope that you've been able to witness your intuitive ability coming to the surface and becoming more prominent. You've likely also seen the different ways it can speak to you and the varied forms it can take with you. As I mentioned earlier, even if you found your ability to be better with some intuitive forms than others, you'll likely find over time and with more practice that your ability with those other forms will increase.

I encourage you to practice using your intuition. It will take regular practice to really hone your ability. If you can, try to carve out some time a few times a week to practice using your intuition, and try not to let a lot of time go by between intuitive practice sessions, no more than two or three days.

You'll find some more advanced exercises later on, and I recommend doing those as well in order to fine-tune aspects of your intuition.

We'll turn our attention next to additional ways to work with and fine-tune your intuition.

seven

Working with Your Intuitive Information

Now that you've been successful at accessing your intuition and receiving intuitive information through the exercises we did in the previous chapter, there are other things you can—and should—do next. This is what we're going to explore in this chapter: what you can do after you've received intuitive information.

Depending on the situation and on the information you received, there are four more steps you can take: interpret, evaluate, distill, and apply. Let's look at each of these steps in turn.

Interpret

Can you always work right away with the information you received intuitively? Well, take a look at the notes you took after doing the exercises in the previous chapter. Does all of the information you received make sense to you? Is all of that information literal, or is some of it symbolic or figurative? Is any of that information open to more than one interpretation?

If all of the information you received is literal, then in all likelihood there's no need to interpret any of it. However, if it's not all literal, then interpretation is critical.

Interestingly, some people may primarily get either literal information or symbolic information. I know several intuitives who primarily receive symbolic information. I'm glad that most of the information I receive is literal, but I have experienced times when the information I received was figurative or symbolic.

Receiving information in the form of an impression may also require interpretation or clarification, which we'll cover later in this chapter. That is the challenge of receiving intuitive impressions: it can be harder to wrap your arms around them and get a clear sense of their meaning.

Interpreting intuitive information can be tricky at times, just as interpreting dreams can be a challenge. Because you're the one who has received the symbolic information, the symbol may contain meanings or interpretations that you would associate with it. However, if you've received the information for someone else—someone you're reading or attempting to get information for—it could also have meanings that the person you're reading for—or even about—might have. This is where the process of interpretation can get really murky. Interpreting information is unfortunately not a straightforward task. Learning how to interpret information can involve a learning curve; however, you can indeed make progress and improve on doing it.

Let's say you have a close friend named Erin who's getting married. Erin knows that you've been working on developing your intuition and she's really concerned about how her upcoming wedding will go. She asks if you would mind seeing if you could get any information intuitively about this. You use the tuning-in procedure and keep getting coins. What would you tell Erin that this means? Coins could mean that there will be a lot of costs, possibly hidden ones, associated with the wedding. Coins could also mean that people will be giving money as a wedding gift or helping to pay for things. Coins could also mean that Erin will have to be innovative in some ways and "coin" some new procedures or approaches to the wedding. *Or* coins could mean all of these things or something else.

Do you see how tricky interpreting information can be?

One thing you can do when you've received symbolic information is to see which interpretation feels right to you. If you do this, you will basically be using your intuition to get a sense of which interpretation is correct. If you've gotten the information for someone else, you could ask that person which meaning or meanings might be right or feel right to him or her.

Another step you can take in interpreting information is to tune in again and ask which interpretation is correct or what the information means.

As you can see, there are several ways in which you can try to interpret any symbolic or figurative information.

It would be wonderful if the intuitive information we received was always straightforward or obvious with regard to its meaning. However, if that's not the case, allow yourself to be prepared to do some interpretation. After all, you want to be able to use the information your intuition gives you, even if you have to take some extra steps at times to figure out what it means.

Evaluate or Ask for Clarification

Why would you need to evaluate intuitive information you've received? It's helpful to evaluate some of the information for many reasons.

First of all, it's almost impossible to be 100 percent accurate with our intuition. Working with intuition is not a cut-and-dried process. Our personal stuff can creep in and affect our information, especially when the subject has to do with something personal or important to us or when it is connected to our beliefs or even what we've read or think we know. Personal concerns and orientations can make information less reliable.

In addition, when studies have been done on psychics—who use the same faculty as intuitives—it's been estimated that the most reliable psychic is accurate about 70 percent of the time, and that's an average with wide variances. As you can see, there is always room for error.

Obviously, intuitive information will only be helpful to you if it's accurate and reliable. So you'll want to take measures to try to determine whether information you've received is accurate. This is where this second step of evaluating comes in.

In order to evaluate the information you've received, just follow this procedure:

Questions to Ask to Evaluate Information Received

- Does this intuitive information feel right?
- Does this information make sense—in other words, does it seem logical (and fit with my left brain)?
- If the information isn't logical, could it still be right?
- Could this information be expressing solely what I want to hear?
- Could this information be coming from what I believe or think to be true?
- Could this information be the result of what I've seen, heard, or read about the issue?
- Could this information be the expression of my fear?
- Is this information usable in any way?
- Does this information help me in any way?
- Can I use this information as is, or do I need to access more information?

Knowing whether the information is accurate can be tricky. There may be times when you find yourself receiving information that doesn't feel logical. However, that doesn't necessarily mean that the information is wrong. As you refine and hone your intuitive ability, you should find yourself more easily having a sense of whether the information feels right or not. If you have any strong doubts about it, you can always tune back in and ask if the information is reliable or not.

In addition to evaluating the information you've received, you may encounter times when you're not sure what the information may refer to or what to do with it. This is where the other aspects of evaluating information come in: you can tune back in and ask for clarification on the information you've received. Likewise, you can always tune back in and ask for additional information.

Do you need to take this extra step of tuning back in with all information you receive? No, you don't need to do this all the time for years on end. However, I recommend that you do try to evaluate the intuitive information you receive while you're still in the beginning stages of learning to access and work with your intuition. After you've been working with your intuition for a while, you will probably find yourself intuitively knowing whether the information you've gotten feels reliable. However, you would be doing yourself (or someone else for whom you were getting information) a disservice if you routinely assumed that all the information you received was accurate. Checking the information with this extra step can be a smart thing to do. I frequently do a quick check almost automatically to see if information feels right.

This step can be simplified over time. There may be times, though, when you're not sure if the information feels right—and it could still be accurate. I've had numerous experiences of receiving information that didn't feel right. When this happens, I often find myself censoring the information.

However, there have been times when the same information kept coming in, no matter how many times I rejected it. When that happens—and the censored information keeps presenting itself to me—I feel that I'm being given the information for a reason and will then share it, with my client often verifying its significance in some way.

The same is true of clarifying what you've received. For example, let's say you receive information about a male giving the person you're reading for some significant information about a project. The information about the male is ambiguous. Is this someone the person you're reading for knows, or is this person a stranger? Does the person you're receiving information for have to ask the male for information, or is it voluntarily given? Clarifying the information you initially received would be helpful in this case, and you could tune back in and ask for clarification.

Initially you may find that you need to tune back in fairly often. Over time, though, you may find your need to do this arising less and less frequently. It's a wonderful step that's always available to you should you need clarification or more information.

Distill

Another thing you may need to do with the intuitive information you've received is to distill it. I say *may* need to do because this step will not always be necessary.

You'll primarily need to distill the information you've received down to its core in two different situations. The first is when you receive a torrent of information. There are times when we'll receive little tidbits of information and other times when the information will be pouring in. There can be times when information pours in to the extent that we receive so much information that it can be somewhat overwhelming. In cases like this, you'll want to distill the information. We distill information when we let it "sift" down and be processed. This is not a conscious procedure in which we distill the information ourselves; instead, we back off and let the information sift down and be processed internally by deeper parts of our mind.

When we do that, at some point the important nuggets of information will become obvious to us, by standing out in our awareness.

We often want to get intuitive information when we're trying to make a decision or gain some insight that will help determine our actions. When we're trying to make a decision or gain useful insight, we may need to take some time between receiving the information and acting on it. The information may need some internal processing to weigh the insights in order to know which course of action to take. For example, if you needed to make a decision on your child's education and some of the information you received was surprising, you would likely need more time to process the information internally. The significant pieces of information would then be distilled and would stand out.

When you take this third step of distilling information, you're not refusing to use the information. What you're doing, on the contrary, is letting the information become even more useful to you.

How do you know whether you need to let information distill? Your gut will tell you whether you're ready to use the information and whether it's been distilled and processed sufficiently.

Apply

This next step is rather obvious, isn't it? Once you know that the information you've received is "ready" or usable, you can then move forward and apply it to the situation or area of your life that it's pertinent to. This is why you've wanted to access your intuition to begin with: to be able to apply it to your advantage in your life.

If you don't know which area of your life the information is related to, you can tune back in and ask that question—*or* you can wait until you have a sense of what to do with the information. In either case, once you know what to do with it and feel good about it, you'll want to use it and apply it.

These are the steps you'll often want to take to work with and use the intuitive information you've received. Once again, they include the following: interpret, evaluate (or ask for clarification), distill, and apply.

Taking these extra steps will allow you to make the information you've received usable and helpful to you in your life.

Try This

Look over the list of intuitive experiences you compiled in the introduction. Can you see times when you applied any of these additional steps? If so, can you see how that might have been helpful? In reviewing your experiences, can you now see where it would have been helpful to use these steps of inter-pret, evaluate, distill, or apply, and you didn't? Make a note in your journal of your insights.

Is this all you need to do to work with your intuition?

As it turns out, there are some additional factors that can help you in cultivating your intuition, and we'll discuss them next.

eight

Cultivating and Growing
Your Intuition

In addition to the how-tos we've covered on accessing and working with your intuition, there are things you can do to improve the likelihood of your intuition appearing to you. Think of your intuition as a plant you are growing. As with any garden, there are things we have to do to cultivate our plants as optimally as possible so they will grow well. We need to amend the soil and make sure there's plenty of light, and then water our garden with the right amount of water, reduce harmful pests and weeds, and so forth.

The same is true of your intuition. The garden your intuition grows in needs to be cultivated in the optimum way to ensure that the conditions are right for your intuition to grow.

What sorts of growing conditions does your intuition need? Well, let's look at what the equivalents of fertile soil, adequate light, and proper water for your intuition would be. Some of these conditions overlap, but we'll look at them individually.

- Adequate relaxation and a relaxed mind
- An open attitude
- Quieting your mind and external noise
- Deeper diving in your mind
- Full immersion/concentration
- Adequate alone time
- Opening your heart to yourself and others
- Observing your thoughts and introspection
- Thinking in images
- Adequate rest and sleep
- Waking up slowly
- Attuning to subtleties
- Using your senses in new ways
- Moving in different ways
- Bypassing personal stuff
- Looking for ways to apply your intuition

If these are the proper growing conditions for your intuition, what would interfere with the cultivation of your intuition? What would the weeds and pests be? The following factors would definitely interfere with growing your intuition in a healthy manner:

- Stress
- Inadequate sleep

- Doubts about your intuition
- Anxiety and tension
- Feeling that you have to choose between parts of your mind
- Getting stuck in one state of consciousness

Let's look at each of these factors in more depth.

Helpful Conditions That Promote Intuition
Adequate Relaxation and a Relaxed Mind

Your intuition will have a hard time growing if you are on the go or working all the time (or at least working a lot in a stressed manner). Your intuition needs a relaxed body and frame of mind in order to sprout and grow. You'll remember that you need those slower brain waves in order to access your intuition and receive information—and that means a relaxed state of mind.

Relaxing your mind and being in an alpha brain wave state can be a wonderful growing medium for your intuition. To know what that feels like, just think of daydreaming or a stream-of-consciousness state of mind, as we discussed earlier. Our lives tend to be very busy and packed full of things to do, which isn't conducive to intuition.

This doesn't mean that you need to be relaxed all the time, just enough of the time. Remember to intersperse your routine with some nice periods of alpha brain waves and daydreaming. Also allow yourself to take intermittent breaks from work. If you ever find the tuning-in procedure to be difficult to do, that may be an indication that you're just not relaxed enough or not getting adequate relaxation a high enough percentage of the time.

Alpha brain waves allow you to glimpse below the surface of your conscious mind. (They serve as a bridge between your conscious awareness and your subconscious and unconscious.) Some intuitive information will spring from these deeper levels of your mind, so this is another reason that you want to be in an alpha brain wave state.

There are a number of ways to seek relaxation. Taking a timeout and allowing yourself to breathe deeply can help you relax fairly quickly, and even more so if you close your eyes while doing it.

You can get a similar effect from stopping what you're doing, closing your eyes, taking some deep breaths, and remembering something pleasant (a situation or an event or a loved one).

Many people find listening to music they like to be relaxing. As it turns out, listening to relaxing music you enjoy can increase alpha brain waves. Which music is relaxing? That is a matter of personal preference. Some people may find rock music relaxing and classical music annoying, whereas others may feel the opposite. So allow yourself to listen to music that *you* find relaxing.

Rhythmic exercises have also been shown to produce alpha brain waves. These exercises include walking, swimming, jogging, etc.

What else can help you relax? How about fragrances you like, whether certain foods or perfumes? In aromatherapy, certain essential oils, such as lavender, are used for relaxation. I personally find jasmine to be a relaxing scent.

Play and games can also be relaxing, as long as they're not too competitive or intense.

Meditation, of course, is a wonderful way to relax and get some stress relief. The more often you meditate, the easier you should find it to get into a relaxed state.

The important thing is that you find the best way for *you* to relax.

If all else fails, just remind yourself to let your mind go on occasion and free-associate/daydream, while also taking breaks from work and tasks. Your intuition will grow well if you do.

An Open Attitude

You want to have as open an attitude as possible when it comes to your intuition. Try not to have any doubts about whether you are intuitive or can access intuitive information. Your intuition will not grow well in a mind that's full of doubts. You want to be open to possibilities.

You also want to have an open attitude about the types of information you can access, as well as the forms in which your intuition can appear. Any doubts or uncertainties, not to mention outright disbelief, about what you can do or how you can experience things will serve as a damper on what you will be able to experience. Those doubts and uncertainties can block you from accessing intuitive information.

If you do wonder about how intuitive you are, try doing some affirmations about this, such as, "I know I'm intuitive—I am intuitive," "Any doubts about my intuitive ability are disappearing," or "I look forward to seeing how my intuition will speak to me."

At the least, allow yourself to suspend judgment about your intuitive ability. You can do this by adopting a "let's see" attitude, which will serve you very well as an enhancement to growing your intuition. If you're open to the possibilities, you will be very pleasantly surprised by your intuition.

As I suggested earlier, it can be really helpful to think of your intuition as a treasure box that you haven't yet fully opened and explored. You might keep this image in your mind, knowing that there's a lot of treasure in there that you still haven't seen and knowing that it's lying there just waiting for you to find it.

Quieting Your Mind and External Noise

Tapping into your intuition through tuning in can yield great results. It allows you to access your intuition on demand, as opposed to waiting for something to come to you or strike you. One downside of tuning in, however, is that it requires absolute concentration. External noise can make it very difficult to do this.

Your inner voice and intuition may speak to you at times in a very quiet and subtle way. Obviously, external noise can interfere with your hearing it or understanding it. However, it's not just external noise that can interfere. So can the internal chatter we tend to have running through our minds on a fairly routine basis.

Meditation and going to deeper levels of consciousness help to quiet that internal chatter and tamp down any internal noise. By doing the previous meditative exercises, you were able to quiet your mind, tune out external noise, and heed your inner mind—at least if you followed the instructions and tried them additional times until you were able to do them. This is another reason why meditation is so important for this method of accessing intuition.

Another thing that I shared with you earlier is that when we close our eyes and take some deeper breaths, we automatically shift our orientation from what is outside of us to what is inside of us, which is very important for accessing intuition.

In order to quiet your mind and tune out any external noise, practice meditating on a regular basis. It may take you a while to be able to shut out any external noise, but over time and with practice you should be able to do this. When I first started doing expos, I found it very difficult to focus because the environment was so noisy, with announcements on the loudspeakers, people walking by and talking, music coming from other booths, etc. However, I found that as I continued to do sessions in noisy environments, my focus improved dramatically over time.

Ideally when you start out, you'll want to turn off any sources of noise or sound. If you can't do that, just keep practicing tuning in, while also meditating, and you should find yourself increasingly able to shut out any external noise and quiet your mind.

Deeper Diving in Your Mind

What is deeper diving in your mind? As you can probably guess, it refers to going to a deeper level of consciousness—those slower alpha brain waves we've discussed. You already know how important that is to accessing—and growing—your intuition.

There's another component to this as well. Because some intuitive information can stem from the deeper levels of your mind, you'll want to become more familiar with the terrain there. I have often been surprised to encounter the number of people who primarily live in—and are only comfortable living in—the superficial level of their minds. Conversation tends to be centered on very superficial topics, such as who did what to whom, who took a trip, and so forth. This type of information can be interesting in moderate doses, but a steady stream of it without deeper topics thrown in can keep your mind's focus on superficial things.

There can be great riches in the deeper levels of your mind, along with that personal stuff we talked about earlier that can contaminate your intuitive information. Both the good stuff and the negative may be found there. You may have heard the term *living consciously*. This refers to living in such a way that you observe yourself—not just your actions, but also your thoughts and drives and fears. Living consciously leads not only to better self-knowledge, but also to greater familiarity with your thoughts and the deeper levels of your mind. All of this is immensely helpful.

In order to live consciously, just observe yourself throughout the day. What are you thinking? What's going through your mind? How are you reacting to events and to people around you? What's pushing your buttons? What's motivating you? If you create a habit of observing yourself in a manner that is fairly light and detached and objective, you'll likely gain much greater self-knowledge.

You also want to meditate on a regular basis, as this will take you to those deeper levels within yourself. Meditation has many different benefits and is hugely helpful with your intuition. This is just another way in which meditation can benefit both you and your intuition.

Full Immersion/Concentration

You'll remember that we discussed the need for concentration when we talked above about needing to quiet your mind and any external noise. Immersion is simply another way of saying full concentration and focused attention. Because information available to you while tuning in can be quite subtle at times, you'll want to give tuning in your full attention and be able to pick up on the smallest tidbit of information coming to you—the slightest thought or image or impression, no matter how subtle or faint.

Simply practicing tuning in can help you to develop greater immersion and concentration, but something else can as well. Can you guess what that is? Yes, it's meditation, of course. The more you meditate, the more you'll be able to focus intently on your inner life and mind. Meditation gives us that gift as a matter of course, as long as we meditate on a regular basis and do indeed get to those deeper levels of consciousness.

So allow yourself to follow that two-pronged approach in order to give your intuition the best conditions in which to grow: practice tuning in regularly and meditate regularly. Your intuition will love it!

Adequate Alone Time

Do you ever find yourself resisting spending much time alone? If you do, you're definitely not alone. Many people are very uncomfortable being alone or spending much time by themselves. However, spending time alone is a wonderful growing medium for your intuition.

When you spend time alone, you may find yourself ruminating and paying more attention to your thoughts. We've already touched on living consciously and how important that is. Spending time by yourself allows you to do this more than if you're constantly around other people—and it's definitely more conducive to observing your own thoughts.

Working with your intuition requires that you focus on your mind (and sometimes on your body, when it picks up on information). Spending time alone is certainly more conducive to this than being around others all the time and having endless external distractions from your thoughts.

You don't have to turn into a hermit in order to develop and use your intuition, but you do want to spend intermittent time alone—and be comfortable doing that. You want a balance between socializing (and looking for external stimulation) and being alone. Over time, as you allow yourself alone time, you'll find it increasingly easier to be alone with yourself. You'll also be providing a much better growing medium for your intuition, because your intuition requires an inner focus.

How much time do you need to spend by yourself on a regular basis? Well, this varies greatly from one person to the next. If you don't already spend time alone on a regular basis, allow yourself to start out with thirty minutes to an hour every other day or every three days, and build up from there. You'll know your optimum amount of alone time and how frequently you need it when you've been around other people so much that you find yourself longing to be alone—and when you find yourself feeling refreshed after having spent time by yourself.

As to what you should do when you're alone, that's completely up to you, as long as you engage in fairly solitary pursuits. You could read, write, garden, meditate, exercise, even watch TV intermittently (but not a large percentage of your alone time), or listen to music. The important thing is that you do it alone and without company or communication with others, so that you can "hear yourself think."

Spending time alone allows us to tap into ourselves and develop our inner depth. This can become a reservoir of strength for us, in addition to creating better conditions for growing our intuition. Author Pearl S. Buck put it well when she wrote, "Inside myself is a place where I live all alone, and that is where I go to renew my springs that never dry up."

If you've never developed or found that reservoir within yourself, you may find it more difficult to grow your intuition. Conversely, the more time you've spent with yourself and the more you've begun exploring your inner terrain, the easier you may find it to tap into your intuition.

Allow yourself to give your intuition that good growing medium and fertilizer that spending time alone will provide.

Opening Your Heart to Yourself and Others
Being a warm, compassionate person doesn't just make you "nicer" and more likeable. It also greases the wheels for your intuition. Opening your heart to others opens you up—and remember that intuition is receptive, in that it's a receiving of information. It's very hard to receive something if you're closed.

I alluded earlier to research done by the Institute of HeartMath showing a precognitive awareness in the heart. Their research also indicates that we're more open to others when we open our hearts to them and feel positive toward them. Does this make sense? If not, just consider being asked by someone you either dislike or don't feel good about to get intuitive information for him or her. Would you find this easy to do? If you imagine a situation like that, you'll likely find yourself somewhat closed to the person.

Let's take this thought exercise a step further. Imagine that this person unexpectedly does something very nice for you, perhaps paying you a compliment or giving you a meaningful gift. Imagine that you now find yourself warming to the person. Will it now feel easier to get information for the person? In all likelihood, your answer to that question would be yes.

You may have found in the past that when you were close to someone, such as a romantic partner or a close friend or family member, you would pick up on things the person was feeling or going through at a distance. This is much more common than you might think. As we covered earlier, when we're close to someone, our energy fields become entwined, resulting in a greater probability of picking up on things with the person, things the person is feeling or going through. We're obviously more open to people we're close to.

Remember this as you work on growing your intuition. If you're doing an exercise concerning someone you don't feel good about, look for something you can like about the person. (There's usually at least one thing!) Find a way to feel warm toward the person. You will find it much easier to access information for the person as a result.

Opening your heart isn't restricted to just doing this for others. It also applies to yourself. Having a warm, open heart toward yourself will have an energetic effect that should make you more open and receptive to your intuition.

Observing Your Thoughts and Introspection

We all have choices in our lives as to where we put our attention. However, your intuition will grow best if you are paying attention to what is going through your mind—not just intuitive information coming to you, but also to your thoughts. Paying attention to your thoughts prepares you to observe and notice when intuitive information is coming to you.

Introspection helps to make this a habit. (Introspection derives from looking within.) So while you allow yourself to carve out alone time on a regular basis, don't just watch TV. Do things that allow your mind to be free to roam and chew on things, and you'll discover the rewards that intro-spection can bring.

Remember that in order to access intuitive information, you need to observe and pay attention to what's coming into your mind (and body). So learning to observe your thoughts and cultivate introspection will also help you cultivate and grow your intuition.

Thinking in Images

It is not universally known that different people think in different ways. Some people tend to think in words, whereas others have a tendency to think primarily in images or even to feel things.

Research has shown that thinking in images or visual pictures may better orient you to having a more receptive mind. As you'll recall, intuition is a receiving of information, so having a more receptive mind lays a better groundwork for accessing your intuition.

Additionally, accessing your intuition is a right-brain faculty. So allowing yourself to think in images, which tends to be more right-brain than thinking sequentially in words or phrases, exercises the part of your brain that intuition appears to stem from.

You'll also recall that intuitive information can be maddeningly subtle at times. In fact, I frequently receive information that feels preverbal. In other words, it's not even close to being contained in a form. Stepping preverbal information down, as I mentioned before, and attempting to translate it into words that can be communicated to someone else can be a little challenging at times.

The more practice you get in thinking nonverbally, the greater the medium you'll be providing for your intuition to grow in. How can you do this?

Allow yourself from time to time to stop what you're doing and try to reframe either the task or something you're thinking about into an image. You can even try to create a metaphor to capture and express what you're in the middle of. When you practice doing this, just ask yourself, "What picture does this remind me of?" You'll recall Forrest Gump's famous metaphor, "Life is like a box of chocolates." You might think of that as an example, if it makes it easier for you.

Allowing yourself to think from time to time nonverbally doesn't mean that you should never think in words or phrases. Instead, you want to do it just now and then (not all of the time) and feel comfortable with it. It will make working with your intuition easier.

Adequate Rest and Sleep

There's no doubt about it: your mind will work best when it's rested and you've gotten enough sleep. Remember that when you tune in, you go to a deeper level of consciousness. If you haven't gotten enough sleep, you may not be awake or aware enough to fully grasp subtle intuitive information coming to you. Even worse, you might find it hard to focus or you might just fall asleep.

It can take extreme focus and concentration to hone in on and pay attention to what's going through your mind. If you're not rested or haven't gotten enough sleep, it's very likely that you won't be able to do this and will miss information.

Furthermore, you'll recall that you can receive intuitive information while you're sleeping, especially while you're dreaming. If you're not getting enough sleep, you'll likely be spending more time in the deeper levels of sleep, which come earlier in the sleep cycle, and less or no time dreaming. Even if you do dream, you may be so tired that you won't recall information from any of your dreams.

How much rest and sleep are enough? Research shows that while most people need seven to eight hours of sleep a night, there are indeed people who need less or more. So you have to be the expert yourself on how much sleep you need. If you frequently find yourself tired or falling asleep during the day, it's likely that you're not getting enough sleep. Likewise, if you frequently or regularly find it difficult to concentrate or find that you can't remember things you did or learned in the previous two days, you may be sleep-deprived, because recent research has shown that not getting enough sleep interferes with learning and forming memories.

Don't look at sleep as a wasteful activity. There are negative impacts of not getting enough sleep on a regular basis, including cardiovascular problems, obesity, diabetes, problems learning and remembering, emotionality, attention deficit disorder, and even a shortened lifespan. Plus, you need adequate sleep for growing and accessing your intuition. It's an absolute necessity!

So observe yourself to determine how much sleep you need—and allow yourself to get it. You'll find some recommendations for how to do that in the section on inadequate sleep later in this chapter.

If you want to develop your intuition to your fullest potential, remember that adequate sleep and rest are vital—and allow yourself to respect sleep for its many gifts.

Waking Up Slowly

If you get information while you're sleeping or dreaming, what happens to that information if you jolt awake and quickly jump out of bed? I'm sure you know the answer to that one. Whatever information is circulating through your mind evaporates instantly when you wake up too quickly.

You'll be able to glimpse and hold on to at least some of the information you receive while sleeping if you allow yourself to gradually come back up to being awake, while lightly paying attention to what is going through your mind. When we fall asleep, our brain waves gradually slow down, descending from beta or alpha through theta and into delta. The reverse happens when we wake up. If you jolt awake, you'll suddenly go from deep theta or delta up to alpha or beta. In order to capture those intuitive gems that were there for you during sleep, you'll want to slowly wake up and gradually climb to waking awareness, while paying attention to what goes through your mind. Lying in bed while you do this can facilitate the process.

As you can imagine, having an alarm suddenly and loudly go off completely disrupts this process. Not everyone has the luxury of waking up by him- or herself without an alarm clock. If you need to use an alarm, use one that plays music (set to softer and not loud or rock music). If you can lie in bed for a few minutes while you gradually wake up, that will also help. Jumping out of bed and immediately thinking of your to-do list will make the information from your sleep suddenly disappear.

If you usually wake up quickly and jump out of bed, this may take some practice. It's well worth doing, though, as you'll be likelier to bring some helpful nuggets back with you.

Attuning to Subtleties

As we've discussed, some of the intuitive information you receive can be quite subtle at times. Yes, it's easier to receive information that's blatant or obvious. However, just because information is subtle doesn't diminish how useful it might be.

Do you pay attention to things that are subtle? Not everyone does. Our contemporary world tends to be loud and jarring, with traffic noises, neon lights, and loud music. We don't live in a world of subtle triggers. We're usually hit over the head with stimuli. Because of this, you may find that you're not that attuned to subtle information or cues. If you really want to grow your intuition and use it to your fullest potential, you'll want to learn to pay attention to subtle information.

You can do this by practicing the method of tuning in. This teaches you to pay attention to subtle information and impressions, primarily because you have to focus so intently in order to be truly proficient at it.

For this reason, I recommend doing the exercises requiring tuning in on a regular basis. You can repeat any of those in chapter 5, along with the advanced exercises you'll find in chapter 9.

As you might guess, meditating on a regular basis will also lead you to develop a greater attunement to subtleties.

So you have two means of increasing your awareness of subtleties and learning to pay attention to them. This is like fertilizing your garden. Your intuition will definitely grow better as a result.

Using Your Senses in New Ways

You might find yourself wondering how using your senses in new ways could help to cultivate your intuition—or even what it means. Well, if you think about it, most of us tend to use our sight the most and our hearing second, if we're fortunate enough to have those two senses intact. If you use your other senses more—smell, taste, and touch—you'll expand your consciousness and experience of life.

In addition, using your senses in new ways will forge new pathways in your brain and add to both your creativity and receptivity. (Do you recall that intuition is receptive?) It will keep you out of habitual ruts that may block your intuition and full awareness.

The first thing you can do to achieve this is to use those other three senses more. When you receive an envelope or package or even a gift, allow yourself to smell it. How about the chair you sit in to read or watch TV? What does it smell like? Or the pen you write with?

You could also try tasting some objects. Obviously you'll want to use discretion in tasting things. You certainly wouldn't want to taste something that might be toxic or poisonous or dirty. But how about other things you haven't tasted, even new foods?

You can also use your hands more to touch surfaces and get a sense of what they feel like. For example, what does the surface of your phone feel like, or your cabinet? You'll recall that touch, or psychometry, is one form of intuition. You can touch objects and receive impressions and intuitive information about them. We're not talking about doing that here, as much as just feeling things to see what they feel like, literally to the touch.

You can also work figuratively with your senses. You could take a situation you're involved with and ask yourself, "What does this situation smell like? What color is it? What would it feel like if I ran my hands over it? What would it taste like?" You could do similar exercises with sight and hearing. You could ask what a tin can would sound like if you listened to it. Working with your senses in this way may feel a little odd, but it should open up your mind and consciousness to new possibilities, which is what your intuition can also do.

The goal here is to push your limits and your patterns by adding imagination and a figurative exploration of your senses. Allow yourself to examine your life for any fairly narrow patterns—and dare to break out of them. Pushing the envelope is a wonderful way to open more to your intuition and pave the way for your intuition to grow.

Moving in Different Ways

Keeping your brain agile will allow you to easily shift mental gears from one state of consciousness to another, which is like preparing the soil in your garden bed for growing your intuition. It will also help to keep your brain young—a nice by-product, don't you think?

Years ago, I heard a neurologist, who was being interviewed on the radio, state that you can help to keep your brain young by using your body in unconventional ways. He suggested walking backward and using your non-dominant hand for activities such as brushing your teeth. Unconventional physical activities will actually forge new pathways in the brain, which is good for keeping the brain young. However, they will also make your brain—and mind—more flexible, which will benefit your intuition greatly.

You can also do other things to move differently. For example, do you tend to be constantly on the go and always moving? If so, why not try just sitting every once in a while?

If you tend to be still or sitting most of the time, why not add some intermittent movement? Getting out of any perpetual physical habits will have the same effect as walking backward.

Remember that your intuition loves openness, freshness, and the fertile ground of possibilities, and that includes how you move your body.

Bypassing Personal Stuff

You will achieve the most with your intuition when the information you get is pure and reliable. If any personal stuff is affecting and contaminating your intuitive information, the information will be much less reliable. This is a critical point and requires constant vigilance.

In addition to tuning in to get information, which I feel is more reliable for bypassing personal stuff, you can always add the extra step of checking the information you've received and asking if it's reliable. We covered these steps in the previous chapter.

So practice tuning in (and meditating) and allow yourself to check yourself. This is important to do not only for your own sake, if you're getting information for yourself, but also for anyone else for whom you're getting intuitive information. You certainly don't want to give others information that's unreliable or coming from a limited place.

You can indeed make progress with getting any personal stuff out of the way. All it takes is awareness and practice.

Looking for Ways to Apply Your Intuition

There are many different ways and situations in which you can apply your intuition. Just as you look for uses for all the new things you learn, you'll want to look for uses for your intuition. Your intuition won't do you much good in life if you're not applying it in some way.

While you're focusing on other ways of cultivating your intuition and nurturing it to grow, allow yourself to keep an eye out for situations in your life in which your intuition could come in handy. If you do this while you're still cultivating your intuition, you'll be that much ahead of the game and ready to bolt out of the starting gate when your intuition has grown and matured more.

Now let's turn our attention to the things that we don't want interfering with the development of our intuition.

Deterrents to Growing Intuition

Stress

Do you find yourself stressed on a regular basis, most of the time, or fairly often? As you know, we live in a very stressful society. Our lives are usually fast-paced, and we often find ourselves trying to cram as much as we can into a twenty-four-hour day.

If you find yourself stressed fairly often, if not most of the time, you may find it more challenging to develop your intuition. Stress is usually the kiss of death for intuition. Can you guess why that is?

As you'll recall, a relaxed state of mind allows intuitive information to come to our awareness more easily. We've talked about the importance of being in an alpha brain wave state in order to access intuition, not to mention the deeper level we get into when we tune in. When we're stressed, we're in a beta brain wave state. This is why stress interferes with intuition: it's a vastly different brain wave state from the one that intuition blooms in.

Just for a moment, allow yourself to call to mind a stressful incident. Close your eyes and remember it, while fully experiencing it. How does your body feel? And your mind?

Now clear that experience out of your mind. Then close your eyes, take a deep breath, and remember a pleasant experience, fully reliving it. How does your body feel now? And your mind?

Can you feel how different those states of consciousness are—and the effects of each one on your body? Can you imagine how difficult it would be to try to tune in to get intuitive information while you're stressed?

Stress is really insidious. It has a list of negative health impacts, not to mention how it affects your mind and sleeping patterns. What makes stress even more insidious is that its effects don't leave you as soon as you unwind or relax. It can continue to affect you by the traces it leaves, such as its effects on your hormones and immune system. You may relax for a while after dealing with stress, but you could get sick within a week or two from the weakening that the stress wreaked on your immune system.

You would probably like to get to the point with your intuitive development where you could tune in and receive information any time you would like, as I'm able to do. Many professional intuitives can do this as well, and you should be able to do this at some point. However, if you're stressed a lot, it's highly unlikely that you'll be able to do this at the drop of a hat and effortlessly, much less well.

How can you reduce the effects of stress? Well, first and foremost, allow yourself to meditate on a regular basis. Meditation is one of the singularly best ways to relieve stress. It's usually number one on the list of ways to get stress relief.

Remembering to breathe deeply intermittently throughout the day will also help to reduce your stress. Taking some deep breaths while closing your eyes will make the stress relief even greater.

Train yourself to catch yourself when you're feeling stressed. Pull yourself up short and out of it. This would be a great time to close your eyes and take some deep breaths, while also focusing on something positive and enjoyable, such as a pleasant experience from the past.

Think about what stresses you. In other words, try to identify both your regular sources of stress and those that have the potential to cause you stress. This can include not just situations but also people you find stressful.

You'll also want to try to avoid or minimize conflict with others to the greatest extent possible. Conflict definitely creates stress.

Allow yourself to truly embrace who you are and build your self-confidence, no matter what it takes to do that (as long as it's ethical and not illegal or antisocial!). People who lack self-confidence tend to be much more susceptible to others, whether friends or family or coworkers, who are critical, judgmental, rude, controlling, or demeaning. Interactions with such people only create more stress for the person who is sensitive or lacking in self-confidence.

This is why it's important to try to find a way to know who you are, embrace who you are, and start believing in yourself. This is also another reason why opening your heart to yourself, which we discussed previously in this chapter, is so important.

Physical affection can also reduce stress because it stimulates the production of oxytocin, a hormone that is not only a stress reliever but also a promoter of health and well-being.

Reducing your anxiety and worry will also reduce stress levels. We'll be discussing this in the upcoming section on anxiety and tension.

Trying to have a positive attitude more often than not can also help. You've likely heard of an "attitude of gratitude," which refers to trying to have a grateful attitude as often as you can. A positive attitude can definitely help to reduce stress. (Trying to be positive and up all the time, however, is unrealistic. Negative feelings can serve a useful purpose, but they should occur a minority of the time.)

Allowing yourself to relax and enjoy yourself will help to reduce stress. Allow yourself to engage in pastimes or hobbies that you enjoy, such as playing games, making things, or spending time with a pet. Whatever you enjoy doing should be relaxing and stress-reducing for you.

There are many more ways to get some stress relief. If you feel that you need more ideas than the ones discussed here, do some Internet research on stress relief. You'll readily find many more suggestions for ways to reduce stress. Once you identify ways to get some stress relief that appeal to you, allow yourself to follow up and do them.

No matter how you do it, you do indeed want to reduce any undue stress that you have, as stress is truly a weed that can hamper the growth of your intuition. Stress is a nasty thing, at times like a virus that can get out of hand. So allow yourself to either nip it in the bud or manage it and minimize it. Your intuition will grow much better in its absence.

Inadequate Sleep

We covered the need to get adequate sleep and rest earlier in this chapter. You should now have an understanding of why adequate sleep is necessary for growing your intuition. If you find yourself having trouble getting to sleep or suffering from other types of insomnia, you can practice good sleep hygiene by taking the following things into account and utilizing these recommendations:

- **Turn off all lights and sleep in a dark room**
  Research in the past several years has actually shown that exposure to light during the sleep cycle results in a higher incidence of cancer (because light inhibits the production of melatonin, which suppresses cancer cell growth). Having any light on while sleeping also appears to interfere with sleep itself. This means that it's best to sleep in a dark room, with no TV or computer on, no night light, and no other sources of light, including a lit dial on a clock. If you have unavoidable light coming into your room, using a sleep mask could be very helpful.
- **Discontinue use of computer and TV at least an hour before bedtime**
  There's fairly new research indicating that exposure to blue light, the type that's emitted by computer

monitors and some phones, interferes with the ability to sleep. Although this research has not been corroborated, there's anecdotal reporting that turning off computers, etc., does indeed lead to better sleep.

• **Take a warm bath before bedtime**

When you fall asleep, your body temperature drops. This is why cool nights are so conducive to sleeping well. If your body temperature is too high, falling asleep may be a challenge. This is where taking a warm bath before bed comes in. When you get out of the bathtub, your body temperature starts to drop, making it easier to fall asleep.

• **Try some relaxing scents**

Sniffing a relaxing scent can also help you to both relax and fall asleep. Thus far, lavender and jasmine have been shown to have a calming and soporific effect. This is a natural and less expensive method to combat insomnia.

• **Use some white noise**

This tip can be especially helpful if you live in a noisy environment or one in which there's a greater likelihood of loud or sudden noises. I've used an air filter while sleeping for several years now in my bedroom. You could also try playing a CD on a loop that has pleasing ambient sounds or use a fan that makes some consistent white noise. Just make sure you don't sleep with a TV on, as the light from it would be problematic.

• **Play some soft and pleasing music**

Similar to the previous method of using white noise, you could play some soft music that you find pleasing and that doesn't demand attention. Many, many years ago I used to turn on music before bedtime that stopped playing during the night.

- **Avoid cell phone use before bedtime**

   Recent research implicates cell phones as causing interference with falling asleep, along with probable headaches and problems concentrating. If you need to use the phone prior to bedtime, a land line would be best.

- **Try drinking some warm liquids**

   Sipping warm liquids—without caffeine—before bedtime could also help you fall asleep. This will raise your body temperature, similar to taking a warm bath, allowing it to more easily drop when you go to bed.

Remember that inadequate sleep is like a plant not getting enough sun or nutrients. Your intuition will not grow well without rest, so try to make sure you always get enough sleep. If you have trouble sleeping and the suggestions given here don't help, you might consider calling a sleep lab, where proper diagnosis could be made and treatment given.

Many people think that they can forego sleep without any repercussions. Numerous research studies in the past several years, however, prove that this is far from true. Consistently inadequate sleep can cause a host of health problems, as already cited. Sleep is truly vital for your intuition as well as your health.

Doubts about Your Intuition

Many people find themselves interested in intuition and would love to develop theirs, but simply cannot believe that they could be intuitive. I was certainly in this category. I was always fascinated by psychic phenomena, but felt that only other people had those gifts. Being intuitive was the furthest thing from my mind, not to mention my self-image.

I struggled when I started working with my intuition because I had never seen myself as intuitive. So I know firsthand how it can hold you back if you doubt that you're intuitive or that you can truly develop an ability with it. Given my self-doubts, I'm fortunate that my intuition developed as well as it did.

Doubt can also be a self-fulfilling prophecy if you don't take steps to manage it. So if you find yourself doubting that you are intuitive or have much ability, please try to change that doubt by recasting it. You can do this by doing one of two things: affirming that you are indeed intuitive, or being open to the possibility that you are, even if you don't know to what extent.

In order to recast any doubts about your intuition, try some of these affirmations:

"I know I'm intuitive, and I'm looking forward to becoming familiar with my intuition."

"I know I'm intuitive in some way, even if I have yet to discover how my intuition works."

"I look forward to uncovering my intuition. I know that it is there and will continue to grow."

You can fashion more affirmations around any self-doubts that you may have about your intuition. If you find any "back talk" occurring when you say these affirmations, pay attention to it, as it will be a clue to what may be causing the self-doubts. You can then create new affirmations to deal with these underlying issues or blocks.

The bottom line is that doubts about your being intuitive prove to be very rocky and infertile soil for your intuition to grow in. Just as you can amend poor soil in a garden and change it to rich soil that becomes a fertile medium, so too can you amend any self-doubts about your intuition and change them to positive and open expectation, out of which your intuition can grow and flourish.

Anxiety and Tension

Anxiety can create the same negative effects on your health—and on your intuition—that stress can, and ongoing tension is another manifestation of stress. Anxiety takes stress as a base and then adds in elements of fear and worry, worsening the effects. For similar reasons as with stress, anxiety and tension will be like weeds in your intuition garden.

As a result, you'll definitely want to get rid of as much worry and anxiety as you can. Knowing how to do that, however, can be a challenge. Doing the best you can in any situation that is causing you stress could lead you to acknowledge that you've indeed done everything you can—and then you can let go of the worry. Worry, after all, often comes as a result of being concerned about outcomes. If you know that you've done the best you can and if the outcome is dependent upon your efforts, then your worry and anxiety should diminish. If the outcome is dependent upon more than your efforts, then allowing yourself to trust in positive outcomes may help. When you've done everything you can, all you can do is trust that things will have a good outcome. This will be easier if you generally have a positive attitude, whether you already have it or need to cultivate it.

Another way to reduce worry and anxiety is by reworking any attitudes that may be triggering these feelings, such as reminding yourself that you are protected and guided and that this is a benevolent rather than hostile universe. Reminding yourself of your spiritual orientation can also help. Believing and trusting that everything happens for a reason can be effective as well.

If worry and anxiety feel more like a habitual pattern for you, then you may want to examine how you developed this pattern and what is at its base. If one of your parents was a habitual worrier or tended toward anxiety, this may have helped to engender your pattern, as you may be unconsciously adopting that pattern and modeling it after your parent's. This is something you can change by first becoming conscious of the pattern and any tendency to slip into worry and anxiety. You can then write some affirmations customized for your particular situation in order to change the patterns.

Anxiety and tension are definitely pests that can spoil any harvest, not just that of your intuition. Removing and re-patterning them should give you many benefits, not the least of which will be fewer obstructions for growing your intuition.

Feeling That You Have to Choose Between Parts of Your Mind

This is a biggie, and we've touched upon it previously.

For some reason—perhaps because we live in an age of specialization—many, if not most, people feel that they have to choose between being left-brained or right-brained and that they can only be one way. This is far from true. I personally feel that it's healthier to develop different skills, rather than focusing on just developing and using one.

Don't feel that you have to choose between being intuitive (which is a right-brain skill) and being logical (a left-brain skill). After all, Einstein, who was famous for his left-brain intelligence, also wrote about his intuition.

You want to use as much of your mind as possible. Indeed, you will always have need for your left-brain skills in life—and not only in life, but also with your intuition. You'll recall that one of the steps to take after receiving intuitive information is to evaluate it. Another step is that of applying it, which involves knowing how and where to apply it. These are left-brain skills.

Thus, using and working with your intuition draw upon not just your right brain but also your left brain. As a result, if you tell yourself that you should be just one or the other, you'll most definitely be stunting the growth of your intuition. You want your intuition to grow and blossom unfettered. So allow yourself to respect all of your mental skills, as they all serve a purpose. You'll be able to grow your intuition to an even greater degree as a result.

Getting Stuck in One State of Consciousness

All states of consciousness serve a purpose. If you're in an alpha brain wave state all or most of the time while you're awake, you'll be able to tap into your intuition, but you won't be able to evaluate the information or know what to do with it, much less get anything else done.

One researcher of brain waves, Dr. James Hardt, wrote that "people who can turn on the ideal brain waves to deal with each and every situation are considered gifted." This means that you'll be at your best by allowing whatever the task at hand is to determine the brain wave state you need to be in in order to accomplish it. For accessing your intuition, you'll want to be in alpha or a high theta at times *while you're receiving intuitive information.* For most of the other steps involved in working with your intuition, you'll want to be in beta. And, of course, while you're sleeping, you'll be in theta or delta.

Our minds are wonderful things. They can do so many different things if we stop trying to put them in a box and force them to be only one way. If you try, for example, to use only your intuition and creativity, you might find yourself stymied by activities that require other parts of your mind, and you'll be limiting yourself. In order to grow your intuition, allow your mind its full range of abilities. That will truly be like giving your intuition optimum fertilizer, water, and light.

These, then, are the things to cultivate and the pests to avoid in your intuition's garden, so you can grow the best intuition possible.

Now that you know how to cultivate your intuition and which pests, weeds, and viruses to avoid, let's expand what you've experienced with your intuition and do some more exercises.

nine

Refining Your Intuition with Advanced and Additional Exercises

Think back on what you've done and read in this book thus far. You've really started to explore and develop your intuition. You've done some initial exercises, you've learned many of the ins and outs of intuition, and you've learned how to cultivate and grow your intuition. You're now ready to do some more exercises, some of which will be more advanced. (Yes, you're ready for them!)

Be prepared, because some of these exercises won't be easy. Some are quite advanced exercises designed to give you practice in bypassing any personal stuff (which you'll recall has to do with your wants, fears, beliefs, attitudes, cultural conditioning, mindset, etc.) that could contaminate the information you receive and make it unreliable as a result. Obviously you want the intuitive information you receive to be as reliable as possible.

Please don't get discouraged by the difficulty of these exercises. Some of them, as I mentioned, are quite advanced. If you find them a little too difficult to do at this point, you can always go back and practice doing the exercises in chapters 5 and 6 again and come back to these later. If that's the case, you'll likely find yourself working your way up to them and gradually improving at mastering them. Likewise, if you find one of the exercises in this chapter too difficult, you can wait a few days or weeks and then come back and do it again.

You'll want to make notes in your journal about your experience with each of these exercises, to review in the future.

Exercise: Bypassing Personal Stuff

Let's start off with an exercise designed to prod you to make your mind as blank a slate as possible. For this exercise, it's imperative that you try to forget—or at the least put far out of your mind—anything you think you know, have already read, or have an opinion about. You want to make your mind a blank slate. This may be challenging for you, as it is for most of us, but it will be helpful for your progress to try this exercise—and, indeed, to do it intermittently in order to improve your ability.

To do this exercise, you'll need to find a topic that's of current concern in the world. This topic could be related to something either newsworthy or controversial in the local, national, or international news. It could have to do with a war, an election, the economy, a social issue, an issue in your local or state school system, etc. It should be a topic for which there is an open-ended answer rather than a yes/no one. You'll want to choose a topic that you've heard about and have even read at least some material about.

You'll need to have the topic in mind while doing this exercise, so don't start the exercise until you have your topic.

Once again, it's critical that while you are doing this exercise, you try to put out of your mind anything you've read or think you know about the issue—and certainly disregard any opinion you may have about it, so you can access pure information that's neither coming from nor affected by your thoughts, knowledge, experience, or feelings. Yes, this is difficult to do, but that's the purpose of this exercise—bypassing what you know, think, feel, or have read.

Allow yourself to get comfortable physically, whether sitting down or lying down, and close your eyes. Start to take some deep breaths in and out, relaxing more and more....

Once you feel yourself relaxed, hold the topic you have selected lightly in mind, and ask what is behind what you have read and what additional information there may be for you. Release the question from your mind and then see what comes into your awareness and in what form or forms....

If you find yourself focusing on anything you've read about the topic or what you know about it or an opinion you have, open your eyes and clear your mind.

Then close your eyes, take some deep breaths, and pose your question again....

After you have received information on the present situation, allow yourself to go to a point in the future—whether one year, two years, or even later—and ask what the situation may be at that time. Clear the question from your mind and then see what comes to your awareness....

Once you have gotten all the information you can, allow yourself to open your eyes and come back to your room, feeling refreshed and relaxed.

———

Were you able to get any information in this exercise? If so, were you surprised by any of it? If you were surprised by some of the information you received, then it's more likely that that information was pure and reliable and not affected by any of your personal stuff.

Did the exercise feel too difficult for you to do? If it did, allow yourself to wait a few days or a week and try it again, perhaps with a different topic.

This exercise is an example of what I mentioned in chapter 1 about being able to gain more clarity and objectivity through using your intuition and honing it. It just requires bypassing personal stuff and gaining clarity.

Don't feel bad if this exercise felt difficult to do. When students in my workshops and classes have attempted this exercise, they've usually had very mixed results. In fact, I've had some students be unable to discern the difference between what they were getting intuitively and their personal stuff, notably their beliefs or attitudes. Other students have been able to bypass a lot of their stuff quite well. No matter how you did on this exercise the first time, you can indeed learn to do this or at least improve on your ability with it.

Learning to bypass your personal stuff takes time, and you'll likely make more progress on this gradually. For that reason, I recommend continuing to do this exercise intermittently, using different topics to focus on. You really should find yourself improving at this over time.

Exercise: Reading a Situation

As humans, we often find ourselves caught up in difficult situations with others, whether a disagreement with someone, a relationship in which we find our buttons regularly pushed, or a work problem or financial issue. Even though we can be extremely clear when we shift to a higher level of consciousness (what some call our soul awareness or higher awareness), our emotional involvement in difficult situations usually leads us to lose that clarity and perceive the situation primarily through an emotional or psychological prism. This is especially true when we're in difficult situations with other people.

This is one reason why most professional intuitives, including those who are quite adept, find it difficult to try to get intuitive information about themselves and rely, as a result, on other professional intuitives when they are seeking reliable and objective information about something they're involved in or close to.

If you can learn how to be clear and objective in accessing intuitive information about yourself when you are emotionally or psychologically connected to the subject, then you will be far ahead of the game and on your way to becoming quite adept with your intuition.

The next exercise is designed to help you develop that ability. For this exercise, you'll want to identify a situation you're in that is pushing your buttons or that you find yourself wanting to get some insight on—a situation that you're emotionally and/or psychologically attached to or affected by. This could be a romantic relationship, a situation with someone who regularly pushes your buttons, or anything similar.

Once you've identified the problematic situation, you'll want to suspend any judgments, fears, hopes, or other feelings while you do this exercise. Your willingness to do so is critical, as it will be necessary for you to be clear while doing this exercise. Allow yourself to be motivated to be clear in order to enter into the right state of mind and heart and receive helpful information.

Hold the problematic situation lightly in mind while you do this exercise.

Get comfortable, whether sitting down or lying down. Start taking some deep breaths, feeling yourself relaxing more and more....

As you relax, find that comfortable breathing pattern that's a little deeper than normal but not so deep that it's labored....

Allow yourself now to see or feel yourself walking outside along a road or path in a lovely place, whether a beach, a forest, a countryside, or some other place. As you walk along, you find yourself feeling completely at ease and comfortable.... You continue walking along, enjoying being leisurely and this lovely place....

The situation you would like insight on comes into your awareness, and you find yourself looking at it in a very light manner, almost in a detached manner. You know that you would still like insight on it, but you don't feel anxious, uptight, or upset about it. As you hold the situation in mind, you see a cloud in the sky—a very big, white, puffy cumulous cloud. You notice that the cloud feels very inviting to you, and you find yourself thinking that you would really like to be able to float along on that cloud.

As you think this thought, you find yourself lightly and somewhat magically starting to lift off the ground, floating easily upward....

As you float upward, you see that you're floating straight toward that inviting cloud....

In no time at all, you find that you're right by the cloud, and you get onto it—by hopping onto it, leaning into it, or any other fashion. You discover that the cloud is quite substantial and fully supports your body. It feels like a big pillow or a huge, soft, squishy marshmallow. You allow yourself to get comfortable on it, either sitting down or lying down, and you enjoy this sensation of floating along on a cloud....

As you're enjoying being on this cloud, your situation comes into your awareness again and your cloud seems to be moving with purpose. You continue to enjoy this sensation of floating along on a cloud....You suddenly have the sense that your cloud is right over the situation on the ground. You realize that from this perspective—on this cloud up in the air—you are able to look down at the situation, watch it unfold, and see it from a much fuller and more objective perspective, including being able to get a sense of what other people in the situation are thinking and feeling. You begin to observe the situation below you on the ground as it unfolds, being fully able to get a sense of what's behind it, the different energies affecting it, the factors of all the participants' thoughts and feelings, and so forth....

After you have been able to get a complete sense of the other participants' motivations and thoughts, you now focus on yourself on the ground in the situation. From this perspective, you are now able to observe yourself—what you're thinking and feeling and how you're reacting—as the situation unfolds. Now allow yourself to observe your own participation in the situation....

Once you have seen and observed everything you've needed to see and observe, gaining more insight into this situation, you now feel that you're ready to come back to the present and to your room. You can now hop or jump off your cloud—and you find that once again you're able to float through the air, this time floating *down to the ground. You continue to float down until you feel your feet on the ground....*

Once back on the ground, allow yourself to walk around until you find a comfortable place to sit. Then sit down and begin to lightly reflect on what you saw and observed—and the insights you gained....

You realize that you'll bring back with you every-thing that's important for you to bring back and leave the rest behind. You get ready to come back to your room, knowing that you'll be refreshed and relaxed. Once you're ready, open your eyes and come back to your room....

———

How did this one go? Were you able to see and observe things you hadn't been aware of—or did you gain any insights you hadn't had before? Did anything you see surprise you? Did you find this exercise really difficult to do, and, as a result, were you unable to observe anything? If the latter is true, as with the previous exercise, you can always go back and redo it in a few days or a week and build up to doing it successfully.

If you were indeed able to observe things and gain some insights, see how you now feel about the situation. Are you feeling different about it now—or understanding aspects of it that you hadn't been able to understand before? When you think about the other person or people in the situation, are you feeling less anxiety or tension about them?

When we're able to do this exercise objectively, we usually find ourselves feeling differently afterward. Our opinion of the people who used to push our buttons often changes. We tend to see them in a different and more sympathetic light. We may even see things about our own contribution to the situation that allow us to change what we may have been doing.

As with meditative exercises, you may find that you moved some energy internally and experienced a shift by doing this exercise. You might find more information and insights coming to you over the next few days or weeks.

This is a wonderful exercise to do to gain insights on and rework difficult situations with other people. You can even vary the scenario, as long as you go to a vantage point that allows you to clearly observe the problematic situation and other participants.

Once again, if you found this exercise difficult to do, just go back to it again in a few days or a week. Over time, you should find it easier to do.

This is another exercise that works on and helps us to improve on bypassing any personal stuff that can contaminate our perception and the information we receive. The goal is to be able to develop and use your intuition without having any personal stuff intrude. You can indeed work toward that with advanced exercises like these.

Exercise: Practice Reading Yourself

We all find ourselves from time to time in situations that are difficult for us emotionally, situations with loved ones that cloud our vision or other difficult situations that can push our buttons, such as those at work or with finances, for example. When we're emotionally attached to a situation, it becomes even more difficult to gain clarity and see things objectively—and access clear and reliable intuitive information. As I mentioned before, even experienced and adept professional intuitives find it difficult to get information for themselves about such situations and will consult other professional intuitives to get the information and insight they seek.

This is not a failing on the part of professional intuitives or yourself. It's because we're humans and we're here to learn and grow. We may get lovely glimpses of other spiritual levels and be able to receive spiritual information, but we're still, as humans, living in human bodies, equipped with limited human minds, and living with emotional and psychological makeups. These attributes are designed to allow us to grow, as they help to stimulate learning and unfolding.

Getting clear and reliable information for yourself can be one of the most challenging applications of your intuition. This is nothing to feel bad about, as it's the norm.

I'm a firm believer in developing our abilities to the greatest extent possible, as well as in seeking solutions to problems and finding a way to accomplish things. I personally don't like to bump up against limitations that serve as blocks. So some years back, when faced with a personal situation that I couldn't get clarity on, I tried something new. To my surprise, I was able to get clear information.

As a result, I know that we can find ways to be clear with ourselves. It's not easy to do, but it can be done.

The next exercise is along the lines of what I tried and did successfully. It's another advanced exercise that could help you in developing clarity and bypassing personal stuff. And, yes, it will stretch you in a good way.

For this exercise, you'll want to think of a personal issue you have that you'd like to improve and that you'd like to receive clear information and insight on. It doesn't have to be a situation involving another person. It can be anything at all, as long as you're emotionally attached to it and are seeking a solution or improvement on it and have felt stymied or frustrated about it.

If you find yourself having difficulty or starting to get distracted while doing this exercise, remember to open your eyes, clear your mind, close your eyes again, take some deep breaths, and try again.

Begin by getting comfortable physically. Begin to take some deep breaths, relaxing more and more....

Once you find yourself relaxed and clear, find that comfortable breathing pattern that's a little deeper than normal but not so deep that it's labored.....

Now bring your question to mind in a light, almost detached manner. Then release it and clear your mind....

Allow yourself to now see yourself as someone else, sitting in a room alone. As you look at this other person, who is really you, attempt to maintain your relaxed state and clarity, just being with yourself and this other person, who is really you.

As you continue to focus on this other person, pose your question one more time and then release it....

Allow yourself to feel the energy of this other person, feeling who he or she is underneath the surface.....

Pose your question in your mind one more time and then release it. With the other person still in your mind, see what presents itself to your awareness and in what form or forms....

After you've gotten all the information you can, thank the other person (who is truly you) and focus your attention on your own body. Whenever you're ready, open your eyes and come back to your room, feeling refreshed and relaxed.

———

How did that go for you? Were you able to see yourself as someone else? If so, were you able to observe yourself clearly and objectively? Were you able to receive some clear information and insight on your concern?

If you weren't able to do this exercise, don't feel discouraged. This is indeed one of the most difficult types of things to do. Allow yourself to come back to this exercise later on and try it again. Over time, you should find your ability with it improving.

Even if you were able to get information on yourself and the issue, I recommend continuing to practice this exercise using different issues and concerns to give you ample and diverse practice.

Over time, and with practice, you should find your ability improving. The clarity and objectivity that you will gain with this exercise should benefit not just you in your personal life but also your intuition, as you develop the ability to become even clearer and more objective with it.

Because this exercise refines your intuitive ability in a challenging way and strengthens your objectivity, it is a very advanced exercise and will take your skill to a wonderful new level.

Okay, you've now completed the advanced exercises. Congratulations—even if in advance—for being able to perform some very challenging exercises! They're meant to help you stretch and develop your intuitive abilities. Do come back to them from time to time, not just to review your experiences with them in your journal, but also to redo them. Doing so will help you develop your abilities even more.

Did you think that the advanced exercises were the last ones? No, I have some additional exercises for you. You'll recall that I've said that you can vary the ways in which you access intuitive information by varying the exercises and scenarios you use. You can always tune in and ask for information in a very straightforward way. However, you can also use imagery in order to access information.

You've already done some exercises that used imagery as a way to tap into your intuition. Those are not the only exercises you can do using imagery. The sky truly is the limit with regard to imagery and scenarios that you can utilize in tapping into your intuition. You can be as creative as you like in devising exercises and scenarios.

To illustrate this, I've got a couple more exercises for you to do that use scenarios that are different from the ones you've already experienced. They're not more of the advanced—and challenging—exercises. They're simply new imagery for you to experience and examples of ways in which you can create your own exercises.

Exercise: Finding an Answer to a Question

For this exercise, you'll want to think of a question you would like to get some information and insight on. It should be an open-ended question or topic rather than a yes/no one. Hold this question lightly in mind as you do this exercise.

Sit or lie down. Make sure you get as comfortable as you can physically. Close your eyes. Start taking some deep breaths, feeling that you're relaxing more and more each time you exhale. If any parts of your body feel tight or sore, feel your breath going to those places as you inhale. Then, as you exhale, feel that you are exhaling that soreness or tightness.

Continue breathing deeply, knowing that you're taking this time just for yourself. Allow yourself to enjoy taking this time for yourself, with no sense of obligation or concerns about things you need to do. This is your time just for yourself.

As you continue to breathe deeply, relaxing more and more, feel your body sinking into the chair, floor, bed, or whatever you're sitting or lying on. Feel your body letting go more and more—and relaxing....

Now find a breathing pattern that's a little deeper than usual but not so deep that it's labored.

After taking some relaxed breaths, allow yourself to see or feel yourself walking down a hallway. As you walk along, notice what the temperature is like here... and the light. Notice any ambient sounds. You're very relaxed, and as you walk down this hallway you notice that there are several doors. Each door looks different from the others.

You continue leisurely walking along, lightly holding the question you have been dealing with in your mind.

As you walk along, you look at these different doors and notice that one of them seems to be pulling you more than the others. It appeals to you more for some reason. Allow yourself to get a sense of which door appeals to you the most....

Once you have noticed which door is pulling you the most, walk over to that door and stand in front of it. As you look at the door, allow yourself to notice what it's made of, what color it is, and what kind of handle it has. As you're standing there in front of it, you realize that there will be an answer for you in this room, even though you don't yet know what that is.

Allow yourself now to open the door. Then walk into the room....

You now walk around this room, exploring it in detail. Allow yourself to feel the temperature in here, the quality of the light, how the room is decorated, what objects are in here. Are there any people in here? If so, allow yourself to talk to them. Are there any papers or books in here? If so, take a look at them, if you feel drawn to do that. Allow yourself to fully explore this room....

Once you have explored the room as much as you would like, turn around and go back out the door you entered through....

Once you're back in the hallway, you realize that you're getting ready to come back to the room you're in, feeling refreshed and relaxed. When you're ready, allow yourself to do just that.

———

How did that go? Do you get any information and insight on the question or topic you had? Did anything you experienced or any of the information surprise you?

Did you receive or experience some useful information? Make some notes in your journal about what you experienced.

You can vary this scenario or even go into more than one room while using the same scenario. You might find guides or other beings in some of the rooms who will counsel you or answer your questions. You can use this same exercise and scenario with different issues or questions.

Remember to use your creativity in devising new exercises and scenarios.

Exercise: Receiving Open-Ended Guidance or Information

There are times when you can use your intuition to get open-ended guidance, without having a specific question or topic in mind. You did some of this in the Initial Guided Meditation in chapter 5, although you also asked questions in that meditation. Being able to receive open-ended guidance is almost like being given a gift that you haven't specifically asked for. The guidance and information should be helpful in some way, and you don't have to put any effort into thinking about what you want to ask. This is what the next exercise is about.

Begin by sitting or lying down and getting comfortable. Start taking some deep breaths and feel yourself beginning to relax....

As you continue to relax, allow yourself to find a comfortable breathing pattern that's a little deeper than normal but not so deep that it's labored. As you relax, imagine a wonderful place that feels perfect for you—whether it's a real place, a place you've been to before, or a place you feel would be wonderful. As this place comes to mind, you suddenly find yourself there. Allow yourself to walk around and get a feel for this place....

You notice how comfortable you feel here. And you're grateful to feel this sense of comfort...and peace.

You walk around a little more, noticing more and more details here, feeling the temperature and hearing any ambient sounds....

Then you have a sense that someone or something else is here somewhere. As you realize this, you suddenly feel a sense of love surrounding you, and you know it's coming from a person or presence in this place. You suddenly sense or know where this person or being is—and you walk to where he or she is....

You find yourself feeling even more comfortable in the presence of this person or being. You feel love and warmth from him or her. Then you hear this person telling you or communicating to you in some way that he or she has some information to share with you that should be beneficial to you. This presence asks if you would like the information.

If this feels right to you, then allow yourself to say yes. The being or person lets you know that he or she can either tell you the information or give it to you in another form, whether written down or contained in an object. Allow yourself to get a sense of which way you would like the information to be given to you, and then let the person or being know....

The being then conveys the information to you. Allow yourself to be receptive and receive it....

Once you have received this gift of information, thank this being.

You may then either continue to walk around and explore this place or get ready to come back to the

*room you're in. Either way, you notice how you feel
after having received this gift of information....*

*Whenever you're ready, you can open your eyes
and come back to the room you're in, feeling refreshed
and relaxed....*

———

Did you receive some information—helpful information? The beauty of doing an exercise like this from time to time is that you can receive helpful information on subjects you may not have considered. It's really like being given unexpected gifts from time to time. You can also vary this scenario in any way you would like.

You've done several different types of exercises thus far, in chapters 5 and 6 and this chapter. Now that you've experienced different ways to access your intuition and different scenarios with imagery, you can create your own exercises as the need arises. As I said, the sky truly is the limit with this. Allow yourself to be creative and come up with your own exercises from time to time.

If you use your intuition professionally with other people, you'll especially want to have a variety of ways at hand to access information. If you find that information about someone else doesn't come by tuning in, for example, you could try another exercise or means of receiving information.

This will especially be true if you use your intuition for others with the goal of facilitating others' growth and unfolding. I not only vary the scenario of exercises with clients, but I also create customized exercises tailored to be helpful to a client at the time. One beauty of intuition is that we can access it in a number of ways!

Additional Recommendations, Cautions, and Tips

In chapter 8 we explored how to cultivate your intuition and grow it in an optimum and healthy manner. The things that will facilitate the development of your intuition will help your intuition to grow well, just as the deterrents to intuition can stunt the growth of your intuition.

I have some more recommendations to share with you, as well as some things to look out for that you'll want to avoid. Let's start with some recommendations. Some of what I'll be sharing comes from my own experience and some from what my students and others have shared with me or asked me over the years. I recently started mentoring others who will be using their intuition professionally. (In fact, I started that mentoring program just as I was working on this book.) I find mentoring others to be very rewarding, and it's also served to remind me of some factors that I may have forgotten about that can crop up as you work more intensely with your intuition. Being aware of these factors should help you in your process of unfolding your intuition.

We'll look at these different factors in no particular order, and indeed, some of them are interrelated.

Preparing for Your Practice Sessions

As you develop your intuition, you may find that you want to tap into it on a regular basis, setting aside time to do so. Do you want to prepare in any way for those sessions?

Some people have a protocol or a procedure—or even a ritual—they go through prior to tapping into their intuition. For example, some people prefer not to eat for an hour or so beforehand, or they may have other dietary restrictions or habits they follow. Some choose to sage their space. (If you're not familiar with saging, it's a way of clearing negative energies by burning sage and wafting the smoke around the physical space to be cleared.)

Some people prefer to light candles or say prayers. Some may want to communicate with their guides or angels or God and ask for assistance and good information.

I don't follow any particular regimen myself, aside from not overeating before a session or drinking alcohol. I also often say a silent prayer before tuning in, asking to be given information useful for my client.

I do make sure that I'm centered. You may want to do the same, especially if you're getting information for a friend.

The more you meditate, the easier it should be for you to center yourself. Interestingly, the more you tune in and use your intuition, the easier it will be for you to be centered and the more often you will find yourself centered. These two should and often do go together.

If you find yourself stressed before a regularly scheduled intuitive practice time, don't worry. With life's ups and downs, we can't always avoid stressful events, but this doesn't mean that you can't tune in and receive useful information. Just do some deep breathing before starting your practice or regular session. As you tune in for the first time in the session, make sure you take some deep centering breaths. The more often you meditate and the more frequently you tune in to get information, the more quickly you'll be able to center, even if you've been unduly stressed.

These are some of the benefits that come from developing your intuition and tuning in. This practice has other far-reaching—and positive—effects that you may not expect or be able to foresee.

With regard to preparing for your intuitive sessions, it's up to you to determine what you need to do. Allow yourself to feel your way along, as you sense what's important for you to do. Keep in mind that your preparation can always shift over time, even if you've been using your intuition for years. You're the one who knows what you need to do, and there's no one way to prepare that applies to everyone.

Sources of Intuitive Information

Many people are curious about the sources of intuitive information, and the question sometimes arises of where information comes from. We discussed possible sources of information earlier, but let's look at this more closely now.

Some professional intuitives feel that their information comes from a particular guide or angel. I even had one professional intuitive challenge me some years back by asking me where my information came from and then pronouncing that it didn't work the way that I had shared. As I mentioned before, I have always felt guided and protected and have always felt a connection to God, to the Divine. As a result, it's never been important to me to determine where my information specifically comes from. I simply trust that I'm either accessing or being given information from a positive source.

It's not required that you have in mind a certain guide or other persona or entity in order to receive intuitive information. This is really a matter of personal preference. Once again, it's important that you pay attention to yourself and your own comfort level. You will know what feels right to you. If you want to personalize the source of your information as coming from an angel or guide, that's perfectly fine. And if you don't choose to do that, that's fine as well. It's really a matter of what works for you. One thing you may want to do, if the source of information is important to you, is trust that this is a benevolent universe and that the source of your information is also benevolent and worthy of your trust. This is something I have always innately known and felt, and it can be hugely protective.

Setting Boundaries with Others

Using your intuition on a regular basis can also highlight the issue of boundaries. We'll be addressing boundaries in more detail later in this chapter when we go through some cautions to be aware of when using your intuition. At present, however, there's a potential issue that you'll want to be aware of as you practice developing your intuition.

You may share with some people you know that you're working on developing your intuition. As others, including friends and family, find out that you're developing and using your intuition—and as you become more proficient at it—you may find them approaching you for information. This can feel like a huge compliment at the beginning, and it is. However, if people continue to ask you for information at odd times and uninvited, it can start to feel invasive. I've had friends want me to tune in and look at something out of the blue for someone else I didn't even know. I've also had mentoring students mention this happening to them. In this regard, working with your intuition is no different from being a medical professional who is approached by others on a regular basis for medical advice.

If this happens—or perhaps I should say, when this happens—you may start to feel assailed and that you have no privacy, if people are frequently asking you for information or continually asking you to drop what you're doing to get information for them. When you find yourself feeling this way, you'll know that it's time to erect some boundaries. I had to train friends that it wasn't appropriate to ask me all the time for information, and you may have to do the same. You can do this in a tactful but firm way and without being rude. You could offer to access information for them at a later time, if you feel comfortable with that. People who truly care about you will understand.

What might happen if you don't erect boundaries? You'll probably find this out on your own, but forewarning can be helpful. If you don't erect boundaries and you do make yourself available all the time, you'll likely find yourself feeling drained and that you have no privacy—not a good thing!

Addressing Increased Sensitivity

There's a potential side effect of developing your intuition that you'll want to be aware of, and it makes conserving your energy even more important as you develop your abilities further. Developing your intuition and opening up to receive information can increase your sensitivity. If you think about it, this makes sense because you're opening yourself up. Your increased sensitivity, whether emotional or psychic, will make it even more important that you get enough alone time, in order to fill up your inner reservoir.

You may also find yourself becoming more sensitive in other ways. You may discover that there are some foods you can't digest as well, or your chemical sensitivity, for example, may increase.

As you continue to work with your intuition and use it on a regular basis, you'll likely notice that you're becoming more sensitive in more than one way. This is really a natural potential result of becoming more intuitive and using your intuition.

You may go through other changes as well. For example, many people go through energetic shifts. Your energy—your personal vibration—may become lighter or faster. This may be happening partially because you're opening yourself up to lighter or higher energies. It may also partially be true because, as you tune in to receive information, you may also find yourself working on personal issues because of some of the insights you get. As we clear personal issues, our energy usually becomes lighter.

As we become more sensitive and our energy shifts, other things may change as well. In addition to food changes, you may find that your taste in clothing changes, or that your interest in some things increases or wanes, or that the types of situations you find yourself in change. Your spiritual awareness may open up and increase. There's no one blueprint for how you may change or what you may find yourself no longer tolerating or being interested in, but there are usually some changes. I'm sharing this with you so you may be on the lookout for these things and not feel there's something wrong with you when you notice changes occurring. There's nothing wrong with you. Changes of some sort are the norm.

Another change you may notice is that you may have a greater need to spend time alone. Time spent alone can enable you to replenish your energy and refill your inner reservoir, as I've mentioned. You may also find that you are gradually becoming your own best authority. Once again, changes are the norm. Even if they feel uncomfortable at first, you'll be able to settle into them over time and will likely find yourself preferring them in time.

Which shifts and changes, if any, you experience will be a matter of individuality. Not everyone experiences changes, major or minor. Usually the changes we do experience are nothing we can't deal with. Moreover, tapping into your intuition and using it as a tool in your life, whether you use it professionally or not, brings so many rewards and benefits that any shifts or changes should seem minor in comparison. Intuition can enrich your life greatly, and that usually overshadows any unexpected shifts or changes.

Cautions and Tips

As you develop your intuition and watch it grow, there are some additional things to consider. Some of these considerations will enhance your intuition, and others will not necessarily interfere with your intuition, but may be related to ethics and principles. I developed this list through working with my own intuition over the past twenty years, as well as through observing other intuitives and my students. Everyone's intuition works in its own way. However, there are some things that can either block progress or further it, and it will be good for you to be aware of them.

We'll look at these factors in terms of don'ts and recommendations. This list is not written in stone, so allow yourself to chew on each one and see how it feels to you.

We'll look at them in no particular order.

1. Don't work too hard at it

You may be very motivated to develop your intuition, which is wonderful. Your desire to develop and reap the rewards of your intuition can lead you to achieve that goal, simply because you're motivated.

However, you don't want to work too hard at trying to develop it.

Yes, there's a learning curve involved—and, yes, we're usually brought up to have a strong work ethic, particularly in the United States. You may have been told while growing up that what you're able to get out of something is directly proportional to the effort you put into it. A strong work ethic is indeed laudable. However, at the same time, you don't want to work too hard at uncovering and developing your intuition.

If you did the exercises in chapters 5 and 6, you have probably experienced how effortlessly and suddenly intuitive information can come to you, no matter how subtle the information may be. All you have to do is get into the "right" state of consciousness, clear your mind, set your inner antenna, and pay attention to what comes to you. This can seem deceptively simple, and your intuition should indeed grow as you continue to practice.

If you work too hard at it, however, it may have the opposite effect and you may end up pushing your intuition away. Intuition is receptive and requires an open, calm, and relaxed state of mind. Working too hard at it can tighten your energy and put you in a brain wave state that isn't conducive to your intuition speaking to you.

As much as you may want to develop your intuition as quickly as possible, remember not to work at it too hard. Don't be a hard taskmaster on yourself or on your intuition!

Instead

Allow yourself to practice using your intuition when you can, using some of the exercises you've already done and looking for situations in which you can apply your intuition—and do this in a very relaxed manner. Try not to push yourself too hard or vow that "I *will* get this right and conquer my intuition." Your intuition isn't your enemy and doesn't need to be conquered. It needs to be befriended and welcomed. Instead of vowing that you'll conquer it, do an affirmation around how easily your intuition will come to you, such as, "I know that I am truly intuitive. I know that accessing my intuition will be easy for me and that I can routinely and effortlessly develop it." Or you might try, "I know my intuition is my ally, and by setting the stage for it to speak to me, I know that it will be there for me."

As we've covered, accessing intuitive information is a receptive function, which means that you need to be in a slower brain wave state that primes you for receiving information. If you work too hard at it, you'll be in a beta brain wave state, which, as you'll recall, does not work well with intuition.

As you practice developing your intuition, allow yourself to believe that it's coming to you in an effortless way. Take frequent breaks as well. Sometimes we'll get useful insights during breaks and spaces between activities.

Your intuition will grow beautifully if you practice developing it intermittently and in a relaxed way.

2. Don't rush or be impatient

There can be a natural tendency to rush when tuning in to receive information, because we may expect that information should come in instantaneously and quickly. As a result, there may be times when you might find yourself being impatient for information to come in right away. If you're impatient, you might rush things and miss out on information that may take a while to form.

This can also happen if you're getting information for someone else who's present. You may feel that you can't take your time because the other person might not be understanding or patient if information doesn't come in right away. You may find yourself feeling pressured to "perform," and in an efficient way.

You'll do yourself a disservice if you rush and are impatient with the process of receiving information. In addition, you might even miss out on some information that way.

Make sure you don't rush or become impatient with your intuition.

Instead

Be easy on yourself by being patient, both with yourself and your intuition. Allow yourself to realize and accept that information may take a little while at times to form in your consciousness. This can especially be true of information that comes in the form of impressions. It may not always rush in.

If you follow the procedure for tuning in (in chapter 4) or use imagery exercises, information should come to you most of the time. Allow yourself to remember this and patiently wait for it to come to you.

3. Don't allow any personal stuff to color information

Do you know why this is a "don't"? I'm sure you do, since we've covered it more than once. You want the intuitive information you receive to be as accurate and reliable as possible, right? As you now know, if your personal stuff affects it, the information you get will definitely not be accurate—or reliable.

This is one of the biggest pitfalls in working with intuition, and many people fall prey to it.

As much as possible, try not to let your personal stuff color your intuitive information.

Instead

As I've shared, the best way I know of to bypass your personal stuff is to use the tuning-in procedure you learned in chapter 4. It will allow you to go to a deeper level of consciousness, while clearing your mind, resulting in purer information. So please use that procedure. I've seen students try to take shortcuts in accessing information, without tuning in to do so, but the information they receive when they do that may not be as reliable. So always use the procedure for tuning in.

Remember that you can also tune back in to check on information you've received and ask if it's reliable or if it has come from any of your personal stuff.

Tuning in will serve you well, if you use the procedure.

4. Don't rely solely on your right brain

Intuition is not the only right-brain faculty. Other right-brain activities include creativity (both artistic and thinking), daydreaming, and feeling, among others. So there's always a potential for using your right-brain faculties so much that you neglect your left-brain modes (logic, analysis, etc.). Despite some people feeling that you should be either right-brained or left-brained, you'll be optimizing your intuition—and your life—by using both.

If you fall into the trap of using and relying primarily on your right brain, you'll be leaving out other valuable modes, not to mention being somewhat lopsided with your mind.

You'll also recall that some of the things you do after you've received information, such as evaluating and applying it, are left-brain modes. So in order to use your intuition to the fullest extent, you'll need to use some of that left hemisphere. Don't rely solely on your right brain, as it will keep you from taking full advantage of your intuition.

Instead

I'll bet that you want to use your intuition as effectively as you can and apply it to as many situations in your life as possible. Am I right? Using your intuition can grace your life in many, many ways, and my wish for you is that you'll discover all the bounty that intuition can bring and develop your gift as fully as possible.

In order to do that, allow yourself to embrace your left-brain faculties. Remember to use those extra steps we covered in chapter 7, including evaluating, distilling, and applying, as those require left-brain skills.

Remember to appreciate your left brain. The faculties of the two hemispheres of your brain are specialized, but they also draw upon and complement each other at times, and some activities require the use of both. Allow yourself to use both of them and exercise them. We have both for a reason. Your intuition and life will benefit as a result.

5. **Don't talk yourself out of the information you receive**

One of the biggest problems for people who haven't worked on developing their intuition is that of learning to trust it. I've had students ask me over and over again how they can learn to do that. They'll tell me, "I know I'm intuitive, and I've had a lot of times when something just told me to do something or not do it, but I don't trust it."

A lot of people find themselves rejecting information they've gotten because of a cultural bias against intuition. Most of us are simply trained to consider intuition to be suspect or unreliable.

If you truly want to be able to use your intuition, it's important to recognize and acknowledge this cultural conditioning—and then decide if you want to be subject to it or reprogram it.

If you do want to reprogram it, so that you can use your intuition as much as possible, then remind yourself that you don't want to talk yourself out of the information you receive that feels right.

Instead

Allow yourself to respect your intuition and learn to trust it. I'll bet that you've had experiences with your intuition that were valid. Those experiences, along with the exercises you've done in this book, should lead you to know that intuition is real and to respect it.

Once you've started to respect your intuition, listening to it should become a lot easier. Plus, the more times you find that you've received accurate information, the more you'll find yourself trusting it. Additionally, the more times you don't trust your intuition and experience negative consequences as a result, the more likely you'll be to start trusting it.

In order to take advantage of your intuition and reap its rewards, you'll need to trust it and listen to it.

6. Don't disregard your gut feelings and bodily awareness

Most people tend to think of their mind and receiving information with their mind only when they think of intuition. Does that apply to you? If so, don't disregard your body. Many people may be fully aware of their gut feelings, but may not even know that other parts of their bodies are just as capable of receiving information.

As I shared with you in chapter 2, researchers have found a scientific basis for gut feelings. Your gut really can perceive and receive information, as can your heart and skin.

So when working with your intuition, and not just while developing it, don't forget to pay attention to how your gut is feeling, along with how the rest of your body feels. Don't fall into the trap of looking for intuitive information to come to you solely through your mind, and, if your gut suddenly feels different (or your heart, skin, or another part of your body), don't gloss over it and ignore it.

Instead

I will admit that I tended to disregard my body and how it felt for many years, unless I had major pain. I've learned to pay attention to how my body is feeling and what it may be telling me. Now that you know your entire body can receive information and provide signals to you, you'll want to remember to pay attention to your body and learn how it speaks to you.

Whenever you practice tuning in and working with your intuition, remember your body and pay attention to how it may be signaling you, whether through gut feelings, chill bumps, heart changes, or anything else. Remember the resource I shared with you, the body communication procedure in chapter 4, to try to consciously capture information that your body may have picked up on.

Your body can truly be your ally in developing your intuition, so remember to partner with it and pay attention to what it's attempting to convey to you.

7. Don't think that you can't develop or use your intuition

Have you ever felt that you couldn't be intuitive? You'll recall that I used to feel that way. Negative beliefs can become self-fulfilling prophecies at times. A lack of confidence can indeed be crippling, and any disbelief in your intuitive potential could block your ability to develop it.

Don't think that developing your intuition is beyond your ability, because it isn't. You don't want to block your intuitive ability by not believing in it.

Don't tell yourself that you're probably not intuitive or can't find or develop your intuition.

Instead

Believe that you're intuitive and can use your intuition! Remember that practically all people are intuitive to some degree, while also realizing that it's just a matter of uncovering how your intuition speaks to you and how it works.

If you find yourself slipping back into doubt or disbelief about your intuitive ability, remind yourself that you are indeed intuitive. You can also do some affirmations on this, such as, "I know that I am intuitive and am fully capable of finding my intuition, developing it, and using it in my life."

No matter how many times you need to remind yourself of this, allow yourself to do it.

Each time you do one of the exercises in this book and receive information, remind yourself of your intuitive ability.

You truly are intuitive!

8. Don't expect to be limited

Some people may feel that they're intuitive, but they may believe that they can experience intuition in only one way or experience only one or two forms of it, or they may feel that they can receive only certain types of information. This is limiting thinking, which can block us from experiencing intuition more fully.

Don't limit what you think you can experience with your intuition. To start on the journey of developing your intuition while feeling that you can only experience certain things is a trap, which can serve as a roadblock to your full expression and development of intuition.

Try not to tell yourself that you are limited with your intuition or can experience only parts or certain forms of it.

Instead

Allow yourself to suspend judgment about what you can access or experience with your intuition. One of the wisest and most productive ways to approach developing your intuition is to suspend any ideas about what your intuition is like, along with any preconceived judgment about what you can experience. Approaching your intuition with a sense of wonder about what lies ahead for you will serve you well.

Here's one way you can do this. We'll use an image I've shared with you before. Think of your intuition as a treasure chest sitting right in front of you that's closed—and that's been hidden from your view. As you imagine this treasure chest, allow yourself to realize that you have no idea what might be in there, but that you know that it's full of treasure, treasure that you'll only be able to see as you begin to explore working with your intuition.

This image is probably a lot closer to reality than you may realize at this point in time. I can tell you that I found a lot more treasure with my intuition than I could possibly have imagined, much to my surprise and delight. The same should be true for you, if you allow yourself to keep a sense of wonder about the various facets of your intuition that lie waiting for you to discover them.

Be open to receiving intuitive information in any form and about any possible topic. That openness will serve you well.

9. **Don't expect to work with only one form of intuition and block the other forms**

Even if you've had experiences with your intuition in the past, you don't want to expect that your intuition will always work the same way that you've experienced it before or that you can only experience the same form or forms of intuition. In other words, even if you've primarily gotten visual images, for example, when you've received intuitive information in the past, don't expect that you will receive only visual forms of information in the future. By doing so, you'll likely be blocking other forms and preventing your intuition from expressing itself to you as fully as possible.

It's perfectly natural for us as humans to build our expectations for the future based on what we've experienced in the past. However, that's very limiting if we also feel we'll never experience anything different from that which we did in the past.

When you invite your intuition to speak to you, you never want to set terms and conditions for it. If you're expecting your intuition to always express itself in the same way or form over and over again, that's tantamount to unconsciously setting certain terms for it and limitations on it. So don't limit your intuition or invite it to speak to you only on your terms.

Instead

As opposed to expecting your intuition to always express itself in the same way over and over again *ad infinitum,* allow yourself to be open to your intuition speaking to you in a multitude of ways, determined not by you, but by your intuition itself. Being curious about how many different ways it can appear to you can help with this. A sense of wonder can also help— wonder about the many faces of your intuition.

I have no doubt that, if you do this, you will likely find yourself very surprised by your intuition. It can have a mind of its own, and a very beneficial and benevolent one at that. Allow your intuition full rein, and prepare to be pleasantly surprised by it.

10. Don't rush decisions and conclusions

As we discussed in chapter 2, your intuition can be very helpful in making decisions—that is, if you don't rush your decisions. One problem so many people run into when they're faced with an important decision is that they feel they have to decide right away. When a decision is rushed, it's more likely that the wrong decision will be made and later regretted.

Your intuition will tell you when a decision is right. If you're impatient and dead set on making a decision before your gut feels right about it, it will likely be a less-than-perfect decision.

The same is true for coming to conclusions. If you rush doing that before your intuition knows the conclusions are accurate, you're more likely to be relying on faulty information.

No matter how anxious you are to make a decision and draw some conclusions, don't shoot yourself in the foot by rushing those decisions.

Instead

As you continue to develop and work with your intuition, you'll find yourself trusting it more and more. Remember that it truly can be used to help you make decisions, because it will know what the right decision is and will probably signal you when you've found it.

Remember, too, that some decisions are complex and that, as a result, we need time to sort out the various factors involved. Some decisions can indeed be made relatively quickly, while others require time for processing, including internal processing. If a decision is important to you, you'll want to take adequate time to make the correct decision, so you don't regret having rushed when making it.

As you intuitively chew on the possible options, you may find that you have a customary way in which your intuition signals you that a decision is right. If so, make a note of what that feels like and how it occurs. This is something you may want to record in your journal.

Your intuition is a wonderful ally in making decisions, so make full use of it.

11. Don't be ungrounded

Using our intuition requires that we enter into states of consciousness that vary from our normal waking ones. Of course, we do the same thing whenever we meditate. Those other states of consciousness can feel really nice, and you may find at times that you prefer them to normal waking reality. As a result, there can always be the potential for us to forget to come back to reality and enter a more customary state of consciousness.

What happens when we stay in those other states of consciousness? We become ungrounded—and when we are ungrounded, we are less able to cope with the demands of our world and three-dimensional living. It's like eating too much candy and then having a stomachache afterward. It may feel good to hang out in those other states of consciousness, but doing so most of the time can affect our lives in a negative way.

Instead

Remember to come back to the present reality whenever you work with your intuition and deeper levels of consciousness. While relaxation is good, work and mundane tasks also serve a purpose in our lives, as do the states of consciousness we need to be in in order to get those tasks done.

You can develop your intuition and use it while also being in the here and now and attending to what needs attention in your life, no matter how seemingly mundane.

Remind yourself to have optimum flexibility of mind, moving with ease from one state of consciousness to another, whether meditative, focusing on a task, or intuitive, for example, and visit each of them on a regular basis.

12. Don't leave yourself open and receptive all the time

As I've shared with you, intuition is a receiving of information. It's a receptive mode. In order to receive information, you need to be open. However, do you want to be open all the time?

One thing that can happen as a result of developing your intuition is that you may become more sensitive, as we discussed earlier. When you combine being open with becoming more sensitive, you can become too sensitive emotionally as well as energetically. Emotional sensitivity, without being controlled, has obvious disadvantages. Being too open energetically also has some potentially nasty side effects.

If you're too open energetically, you can let in some discordant or unpleasant energies that can affect you. You might find yourself feeling down or out of sorts for no reason, as a result of having let in someone else's energy who's been feeling that way. You could also find yourself feeling drained.

While it's important to be open while receiving intuitive information, you don't want to be open or receptive all the time—for the sake of your health and well-being.

Instead

Learn to erect boundaries. It's very important to find a way to do that when you're working with your intuition and to figuratively "close the door" after you've finished tuning in and receiving information. I will admit that this can be easier said than done at times.

Erecting boundaries is not a matter of flipping an on/off switch, so I can't give you an exercise to use that will instantaneously create a boundary. I myself struggled with being too open for a few years after I started doing readings. I even had some clients tell me that I was too open and wasn't putting up protective boundaries. This made no sense to me at the time, as I wasn't that knowledgeable about boundaries and quite frankly wasn't convinced that I needed them. A few years after I started working with my intuition, though, I started getting sick over and over again with nagging little bugs. The light bulb went off, and I realized that my chronic sickness was due to a lack of boundaries.

So how can you erect some boundaries to protect yourself from being too open and picking up on negative energies?

Here's what I recommend.

First of all, think back to the Initial Guided Meditation we did in chapter 5. Do you recall my asking you to make a note of how you felt after doing that meditation? If you don't immediately remember how you felt, take a look at your notes. Did you feel really calm and like nothing could bother you? This is what it feels like to be centered.

You'll want to be able to consciously remember that feeling of being centered at will. It's one part of working on establishing boundaries.

The next thing you want to do is to meditate on a regular basis, so you can feel centered and calm more and more often. This is very important and shouldn't be downplayed.

You'll also want to make a decision to value this feeling of being centered—and to value it enough not to let anything pull you out of your center. An intrinsic part of doing this is to realize and affirm that you deserve to have a sense of sanctity and not feel drained. This is critical, because without deciding that you deserve to have boundaries, you certainly won't be able to erect them.

The next step is to pay attention to how you feel when you're around other people. Notice the slightest pull of anyone on you that starts to pull you out of your center. Notice if you feel tired around anyone or after having spent time with any particular person. If you feel any of that, energetically "back up" and withdraw your energy. You may want to visualize being encased in a bubble or a wall going up between the other person and you.

You'll also want to do this when you're getting information for other people, if you do get information for others at some point, whether friends, family, or clients. You'll want to consciously open yourself up to the other person, while discerning the quality of energies you experience and not letting any discordant ones in to affect you. After you finish receiving information for the other person, you'll want to figuratively close your "door" and energetically back up if you feel any pulling on your energy.

Meditating after receiving information for someone else and tapping back into the pure energy of your center can also cleanse and refresh you, while seating you back in your center. Of course, using the method of tuning in as a means of accessing your intuition will also help to center you.

Once again, establishing boundaries is not as simple as flipping a switch. It requires practice, and you should see improvement over time if you work on it regularly. The more often you find yourself in your center and experience how wonderful and powerful that feels, the more prepared you'll be for not letting yourself be pulled out of it. Meditation is one of the best ways I know of to find your center. This is just another in a long list of benefits that you can derive from meditating and is why meditation is so important to do on a regular basis.

In addition to these suggestions, you might also look at whether you're susceptible to any old programming around not deserving to feel safe or centered, as that can predispose you to neglect establishing boundaries or not feel worthy of having them or to feel guilty if you do have them. If there are any old tapes playing in your head or beliefs like that, allow yourself to deprogram them. Doing an affirmation may help with this, such as, "I know I deserve to feel safe and centered and am worthy of having boundaries." Be sure to do any affirmations regularly—twice a day, in the morning and at bedtime—until the old programming has been replaced. If you detect any self-backtalk (negative responses from your unconscious) while doing affirmations, pay attention to it and then do some new affirmations to counter the negative responses. (Backtalk usually indicates underlying issues that are blocks, and paying attention to it allows you to identify the blocks for clearing.)

We truly can be compassionate toward others without opening ourselves up to being drained. You should not feel any guilt about erecting boundaries.

13. Don't allow yourself to be overwhelmed by stimuli

This goes hand in hand with the previous cautions about not being too open and not having overly thin boundaries. If you become too sensitive or stay open for too long, you may find yourself bombarded by external stimuli. This can be quite draining as well as distracting.

Instead

If you want to get reliable and quality intuitive information, find a way to focus and shut out external stimuli.

Fully developing and using your intuition requires focus and concentration, especially while tuning in. Information may suffer in quality and reliability if you're distracted while tuning in, as the distractions will interrupt you and the flow of information, as well as disturb your level of consciousness.

Admittedly, finding a way to not be distracted by what's going on around you, especially if there are sudden and/or loud noises, is not easy to do. When I first started doing mini-readings at expos, I was taken aback by all the noise, as I shared earlier. At unexpected times, the loud speakers would crack to attention and a blaring voice would start making announcements. It was very hard to focus and concentrate under those circumstances.

However, I kept doing expos and I found that over time my ability to focus and concentrate, even with loud noise erupting unexpectedly, grew and grew. It just took practice, and I gradually developed the ability to tune out external distractions while I tuned in to receive information.

Even though you may find external noises and other stimuli to be distracting while you're trying to tune in, you can develop the ability—over time—to tune out those distractions. It just takes practice in tuning in.

If you find yourself distracted by noise or other stimuli before you've built up the ability to tune them out, then just open your eyes, take a deep breath, close your eyes, and tune in again, because information received while you were distracted may not be accurate or may be incomplete.

As you continue to practice tuning in on a regular basis, you will find yourself more and more able to avoid being distracted by what's going on around you.

14. Don't heed negative input or pooh-poohing from others

One of the challenges in developing and using your intuition is learning to trust it. This process can involve a learning curve, and, while you're still involved in that process, feeling supported by people around you can make that process easier. Conversely, having people close to you not be supportive can impede your progress and make you doubt yourself.

Unfortunately, some people may be negative or sarcastic about others' attempts to use their intuition. If you have people like that around you, be very careful not to listen to any negative feedback from them. Do not heed anyone if you hear them pooh-poohing you and your attempts to access, refine, and use your intuition.

There are times when it serves us best to listen to ourselves and to not heed negative things that others have to say to, for, or about us. This is one of those times.

Instead

If you truly want to develop your intuition and use it as a tool, it's imperative that you shut out anyone who tells you that you can't do it, or that intuition is nonsense, or that the information you receive can't possibly be true.

Allow yourself to ignore any naysayers in your life, regardless of how well intentioned they might be or how close they are to you.

Shut out any negative feedback from others who doubt either your ability or intuition itself. Instead, simply trust in your intuitive capability and what your intuition has to tell you.

15. **Don't give unsolicited advice or information to others**

One potential trap in developing your intuition is the feeling that other people need you to give them information. It may be true in some instances that some people do need this, especially if you begin to work professionally with your intuition.

However, it is not true that, just because you have learned to access intuitive information, you need to give information to others without their having asked for it. Approaching someone and telling them you have information for them, when they haven't asked you for it, is intrusive. (I have experienced others doing this over the years and can attest to how intrusive it feels.)

Don't accost people you don't know and give them unsolicited information.

Never assume that others want any information you have accessed intuitively when they haven't asked for it.

Don't give unsolicited information or advice to someone you do know, unless you have their permission to do so or they have asked you for it.

Instead

Give information or advice only when asked to. Make sure that you respect others' boundaries and privacy in sharing information you have intuitively received. Only share information if you've been asked to do so.

Always ask permission of someone before you even attempt to get intuitive information that may concern him or her. Allow yourself to respect others' boundaries and right to privacy and feeling of sanctity. The only exception to this would be a life-or-death situation in which your intuitive information could save a life or avert harm.

Other than in emergencies, allow yourself to respect the privacy of others and their boundaries.

16. Don't think that you know what's best for others

Another potential pitfall for some people in developing and using their intuition is the development of an attitude that they're privy to insider information—and that, as a result, they know what's best for others or how others should live their lives.

It's important to realize that being able to use your intuition does not endow you with insider knowledge about how others should live their lives. Never assume that you know what's best for other people.

Don't be tempted to think that you know how others should live their lives. When we have the attitude that we know better than others how they should live their lives, we are viewing them in a diminished fashion and usually as smaller or less than us, or as needy and/or dependent. This is a very disrespectful attitude.

Never tell others that you know what they should do better than they do, and don't tell others how they should live their lives.

Instead

Respect the rights and privacy of others to live their own lives. It's very important to maintain respect for others—and to remember and respect their right to privacy and independence. Remember that others are discrete people unto themselves with their own autonomy and are worthy of respect for their ability to manage their lives.

If you find yourself tempted to tell someone what he or she should do based on intuitive information that you've received, just bite your tongue and remind yourself of the previous statements.

When sharing information—if you've been asked to do so—phrase it in a noninvasive and non-dictatorial fashion. For example, instead of saying, "You shouldn't do such and such," say, "I'm getting that such and such may not be the best approach or that it could be counterproductive or that it may not be helpful." You could also share the results of the actions you're getting that aren't helpful, as long as you have intuitively received those results of the actions.

We can convey useful intuitive information to others without stepping over the line of telling them how to live their lives.

Have in your mind at all times that you are aware of and respect others' ability to make wise choices for themselves, as well as to learn from any "mistakes" or difficult experiences in their lives.

17. Don't expect others to be dependent on you

This is somewhat related to numbers 15 and 16. However, it is significantly different enough to warrant its own listing.

There can be a tendency for some people who have developed their intuition and who are using it somewhat fluidly—and who frequently get information for others, whether in a professional capacity or not—to unconsciously either expect or want others to be dependent on them as a result. This may happen as a result of feeling so gratified when others appreciate their intuitive information that their abilities go to their head and they get an ego boost as a result. That ego boost can possibly lead to craving the feeling of power that results from having others depend on them.

If you find yourself feeling an out-of-the-ordinary ego boost when others praise your intuitive abilities, don't allow this gratifying feeling to lead you to want others to become dependent on you. Dependency is evident when clients (or friends, if you're getting information for them) increasingly look to you for information on decisions they're trying to make and forget to think for themselves.

Doing so creates harm both to yourself and to the other person and blocks a healthy, on-an-equal-par relationship, while inhibiting the other person from being independent and thinking for him- or herself.

Don't be tempted to encourage others to become dependent on you as a result of your accessing intuitive information. You don't want to prevent others from thinking for themselves. Don't allow yourself to fall into the trap of needing others to be dependent on you.

Instead

Know that it's always best for others to develop a healthy self-reliance and to make their own decisions, even if you have to remind yourself of this.

One goal of your accessing intuitive information for others is that of empowerment, not dependence.

If you find yourself wanting clients and others to need you in place of thinking for themselves, try to curb this tendency. Be on the lookout for this pitfall, should it manifest in your life.

Remember that you are only sharing information you have received, rather than setting yourself up as a parent or guardian or guru.

Encourage others' growth and movement toward empowerment, including toward their own development of intuition.

Set and maintain healthy boundaries and mutual respect.

18. **Don't let your intuitive ability lead you to feel grandiose**

Being able to access and utilize intuitive information is a wonderful thing. It's a skill that can benefit us greatly in our lives, as I've stated over and over again and as I'm sure you know. However, we have to look out for any possible temptation that could stem from developing our intuition in order to feel that we're "special" or better than others.

Don't allow yourself to feel that you are one of the few people in the world who are either intuitive or able to receive valid intuitive information. Don't be tempted to see yourself as a special person as a result of your mastering your intuitive potential.

Don't fall into the potential trap of seeing yourself as a guru or as better than others as a result of having learned how to access and use your innate intuitive ability.

Instead

Retain your humility. It can be helpful to remind yourself that practically everyone indeed has intuitive ability and potential, even if it lies dormant in so many. In actuality, if information is energy, then we all have an equal ability to tap into and access it. In this way, intuition can be quite democratic in its accordance of "special" abilities.

It is true that some people may be able to access deeper spiritual information or higher-level spiritual truths. (Valerie Hunt touched upon this in her excellent book *Infinite Mind*.) Not everyone, however, is either spiritual in orientation or spiritually wise or attuned to a higher spiritual level—and receiving intuitive information does not automatically make one spiritually wise or spiritually adept. That said, everyone has the ability to access intuitive information, even if it is untapped.

Remember that a healthy dose of humility can often reveal a wiser nature and a more advanced level of personal development than grandiosity—and that we all have much to learn and can always grow while we're still here on this planet.

19. Don't obsess

There can be a natural tendency while we are in the process of learning a new skill, especially one that we consider to be highly desirable, to obsess over it. However, you don't want to focus so much on your intuition that you begin to virtually eat, sleep, and drink intuition.

Don't obsess about intuition to the point where it's uppermost in your mind most of the time.

Don't allow yourself to interpret everything in your life in terms of or from the standpoint of intuition.

Don't focus so much on intuition that you neglect other parts of your life, such as work or relationships, or stop using other aspects of your mind, such as your left-brain modes of analysis, logic, deduction, etc.

Intuition, when well-developed, can fit into and complement other areas and parts of our lives, which is wonderful. It's a very useful tool that can enhance other parts of our lives, but it shouldn't supplant or replace those parts or become the centerpiece of our lives. Obsessing over it tends to make it primary in our lives and cast a shadow over the rest.

Instead

Maintain balance in your life and assign intuition an appropriate place in your life. Accessing intuitive information is only one of your mental abilities, and your other mental modes serve very useful purposes as well.

Don't obsess about developing your intuition to the point where you're working at it too hard. If you work at it too hard, you'll likely end up pushing it away, as mentioned previously.

Your intuition and intuitive abilities will indeed grow over time, but, just like a watched pot of water, they do not need you to keeping them uppermost in your mind constantly or continually supervised or monitored in order to develop. So allow yourself to take breaks from working on your intuition and from thinking about it. It's important to put your intuition out of your mind from time to time and focus on other aspects of your life.

20. Don't ask the same question over and over again

There may be times when you're trying to get intuitive information for yourself about a subject that you're emotionally attached to. (As you'll recall, this is far from easy to do.) This could be about a romantic relationship, a problem with your job, or any other topic that has you emotionally attached to the outcome. Because you're emotionally attached to the issue, you may find yourself dissatisfied with the information you receive and then find yourself asking the same question over and over again. This is nothing to feel bad about, as it's something we may all be tempted to do.

That said, try not to be tempted to ask the same question repeatedly in an obsessive manner. Doing so will frequently result in getting increasingly unhelpful information or even nonsense. When this happens, it's almost as if the universe or your guides are chiding you and telling you to stop by giving you nonsense information.

Don't succumb to the temptation to ask the same thing over and over again.

Instead

A good rule to follow is to not ask the same question more than twice if you are emotionally attached to it. This takes discernment, but the truth is that we usually know when we're emotionally attached to a subject. We may worry about the outcome or find it hard to put the problematic situation out of our minds. When you know that the question you're seeking to get intuitive information for is one that you're emotionally attached to, remind yourself of this fact.

If you get information on your question and find yourself dissatisfied with the answer, you can try a second time to receive information. If you find yourself dissatisfied again, remind yourself that this is a time to wait before seeking more information—meaning waiting a day or so before asking again.

Before seeking to receive information again on the same question, make sure that you wait a day or two. In time, more information that you can use should come to you if you're clear and are bypassing your personal stuff.

21. Don't look for meaning everywhere and in everything

Sometimes when we begin to work with our intuition, we find it so enjoyable that we look everywhere for both information and meaning. This can be especially true with synchronicity. Synchronicity may be defined as the simultaneous occurrence of events that are unrelated but appear to have a common thread or to be giving us meaning. (The scenario in chapter 1 with Sherry, who was in an abusive relationship and eventually sought help at a women's shelter, highlighted that.) When we encounter seeming synchronicities, we may find ourselves asking, "What does that mean?"

Finding true meaning in things is rewarding. However, not everything has meaning that is hugely significant, and we can go overboard looking everywhere for meaning and end up wearing ourselves out. If you find yourself looking everywhere for meaning, it's tantamount to working too hard. If there's meaning for you in events, your intuition will tell you so.

Don't look everywhere for earth-shattering meaning or feel that everything is giving you an important message.

Instead

Learn to discern what is meaningful and what isn't. There is indeed a learning curve involved with using and applying your intuition, and you don't want to turn over every figurative rock in your life and examine every situation for meaning.

Yes, you will find meaning in some events and situations, but not everywhere. Discernment can also be an important aspect of developing your intuition, so practice determining whether information has significant meaning for you, including with synchronicities. Your discernment of what is truly meaningful and significant will develop and increase over time, and your intuition can help your discernment grow.

Be gentle and patient with yourself as you acquire this skill.

Allow your gut and inner knowing to steer and guide you toward knowing what is truly meaningful.

22. Don't forget your ethics and principles

Don't see intuition and your development of it as something that is separate from the rest of your life. Just as some people may leave their ethics and principles at the door when conducting business by telling themselves, "Well, this is business," you don't want to find yourself having that attitude with your intuition and divorcing it from your conscience.

Intuition is indeed a part of your life, and you don't want to separate your values and principles from it. Just as cheating someone out of money or lying to get ahead in your career would be viewed as unethical, so too would similar actions when using your intuition.

Unfortunately, there are some people using their intuitive skills professionally who do forget their principles. There are many accounts of people having been cheated out of a lot of money by psychics who told clients they had a curse on them and the psychic could remove it for a large sum of money. Similarly, you wouldn't use your intuitive ability to get information unethically and without permission about a rival in order to advance yourself—if you have good principles and strong ethics.

These are just two examples of unethical practices, but there are many other ways we could overlook our principles when using our intuition. It's never a good thing to divorce your ethics from your use of intuition.

Instead

Allow yourself to honor the principles and values you have, and remind yourself that you want to have as clear a conscience when using your intuition as you do in living the rest of your life.

Embrace your ethics and principles when using your intuition, both for yourself and for others. The more ethical you are, the more respectable you will be and the clearer your conscience will be.

Try This

Allow yourself to look over your list of intuitive experiences. After reviewing the cautions and tips in this chapter, determine whether you've experienced any of them, and make a note of each experience that you remember.

Now review what you noted. Are there any cautions that show up several times? If so, make a note of which ones are prominent and have recurred. You may want to find a way to avoid them by reviewing the corresponding recommendations.

Are there any of the positive recommendations that show up several times? If so, congratulations! Consciously acknowledge them—and keep doing them.

Remind yourself that you can improve on any "don'ts" and that you can continue to make progress until you are experiencing primarily just the positive tips.

Final Thoughts

You've been on quite a journey in this book, exploring and working on your intuition. You will reap great rewards from developing and using your intuition and making it a part of your life. Allow yourself to remember that joy, and don't focus on "working" on your intuition.

As you've learned, different intuitives may specialize in getting different types of information. We touched upon this earlier, and it's important to underscore it here. Some people may primarily get precognitive information about things that will happen in the future. Others may specialize in finding missing persons or objects. Still others may focus on communicating with passed-on loved ones. I've been fortunate to receive information on many different types of things and have yet to find a general type of topic or question that I can't receive any information on. I feel it was good that I first started doing readings on a 900 line, as that gave me practice in looking at a wide range of issues and in receiving many different types of information. In spite of my experience with and ability to get different types of information, I feel that my greatest gift (and the focus of my work) lies in reading people—their essence, purpose, life path—and helping them unfold and grow.

It's important to note that when I first started, I had no preconceived notions about the type of intuitive information I would specialize in. I hadn't even theorized about "essence," or people having an innate essence, separate and apart from their soul. In fact, it took me three or four years to begin to figure out that I was reading the essence of clients.

The lesson from my experience? Don't start out feeling or believing that you already know what type of information you will be focusing on or be best at receiving. Developing your intuition is a process—but so is working with your intuition. As you work with your intuition over time, you'll experience ebbs and flows and find new facets of your intuition appearing along with new gifts. If you maintain an open attitude about what you can do, you may be very pleasantly surprised by how your intuition unfolds and what you find you can do with it.

This doesn't mean that you will be able to receive intuitive information on everything all the time. I have been very fortunate to have received information most of the time. However, there have been those rare occasions when I attempted to receive information on a question I was asked—and nothing came in. I was quite surprised the first time this happened, and have had it happen a few more times over the years.

Why does this happen? I have no idea. The point is that there may be times when you may ask something and tune in, but the information doesn't come. Fortunately, this seems to happen very infrequently, but it does happen. If you find it happening, please don't feel that you have failed, as you haven't. Accessing and receiving intuitive information is an inexact science, and you will encounter anomalies from time to time.

Please remember, too, that you will not be 100 percent accurate with the information you receive. There are times when I feel that we receive the information we're supposed to receive. We may be meant to go down a certain path for the experiences we will have that we will learn from. If we always knew in advance what would happen in our lives, there would be no learning, growing, or unfolding. So don't get personally or emotionally attached to feeling that you either are or should be accurate all the time. Not only is that well-nigh impossible, but you would also be misleading yourself and disappointed. It's important to trust that you're doing the best you can and receiving the information you're supposed to receive.

You now have a lot of information about intuition and have taken steps to begin to develop yours. If you'd like to develop your intuition further, you'll want to practice tapping into it and applying it on a regular basis. It would be helpful to practice using and applying it at least a few times a week. However, remember not to overdo it. You want to be in the driver's seat with your intuition and not have it either control you or define everything else in your life. Intuition is a marvelous tool for you in your life, but it doesn't take the place of your life. You can develop and hone your intuition while also enjoying the rest of your life.

Remember to keep a journal of your experiences with your intuition and review it from time to time. Doing so should allow you to notice the progress you're making and consciously remind you of your growing accuracy and expanding ability.

I encourage you on this path, and I know that your intuition will develop beautifully for you. Enjoy the process!

Working with Your Dreams

Our dreams can be a wonderful source of information, some of it intuitive and some of it containing other types of insights. The challenge in using the information, of course, is figuring out what it means, since our dreams can seem so mysterious and downright bizarre at times. No matter how bizarre they may seem, our dreams will still often have important insights to give us.

I've been fascinated by dreams and our sleeping world for many years. Aside from the fact that I love to sleep and be somewhere else, I'm also a firm believer that our dreams can give us great gifts. They are a rich source of insight that we can use for our personal process and unfolding in life, not to mention our spiritual life. I've been interpreting others' dreams for many more years than I've worked with my intuition and have seen clients over and over again have the light bulb go off when they finally grasp what a significant dream meant. Dreams are one of my favorite topics, and I've written, spoken, and been interviewed numerous times about them.

Through my years of working with both my dreams and clients' dreams, I know firsthand that working with your dreams can enhance your life. Dreams can be such a very rich source of information and realizations for us that we often don't or can't get from other sources.

Not all of that information, however, will be intuitive. While some dreams can present us with intuitive information, not all dreams do. In fact, intuitive dreams may represent a minority of the dreams we have.

While I could share reams of information with you about dreams, in this appendix I'll share just some of the basics about dreams, to enable you to begin to decode the meanings of your dreams.

Facts about Dreams

Let's start off with a few facts about dreams. These factoids are based on questions I've frequently been asked when I've spoken on dreams, been interviewed, or held seminars on the subject, as well as from my decades-long love of sleep and dream research:

- *Does everyone dream?*

    Yes, just about everyone dreams, unless there's a personality abnormality or even medications interfering with it. We only remember our dreams, though, when our level of consciousness shifts while we're dreaming, perhaps to shift position or because we heard a noise.

- *Can you learn to remember more dreams?*

Yes, you can. In order to do this, you have to really *want* to remember your dreams. Remind yourself when you go to bed that you want to remember your dreams. This may take some practice, but if you do this over a period of time, you should begin to remember them. In addition, make sure that you get enough sleep on a regular basis, as inadequate sleep can interfere with remembering your dreams.

- *Should I interpret or keep a dream journal of every dream I remember?*

Keeping a dream journal can be a useful practice, as you can go back intermittently and reread dreams you made a note of months before. Often when you do that, you may find yourself knowing more or having a better sense of what a dream was telling you. However, I don't recommend recording or interpreting every dream you remember, because not every dream will be significant. You'll want to interpret only the significant dreams you've had.

- *How do I know whether a dream is significant?*

Significant dreams can affect us in ways that signal to us that they were important. When a dream is significant, we may not be able to get it out of our mind, we may be very struck by it, it may elicit strong emotions in us, or it may reverberate or echo in our minds over the following day or two.

• *What are recurring dreams?*

Recurring dreams are dreams that we have over and over again, whether during a fairly short period of time or over months or even years. Usually a recurring dream is trying to give us a message. These messages can be about issues we're dealing with currently in life, events that will happen in the future, or even past-life events or issues that are affecting us in the present lifetime. Recurring dreams can also shift and change and evolve over time.

• *Why are dreams so bizarre?*

Most, but not all, dreams stem from our unconscious, and our unconscious works in a very different manner from our conscious mind and has a very different "vocabulary." Our unconscious tends to work by free association and even puns. As a result, it will express itself in our dreams through imagery and symbols, including really bizarre ones that leave us scratching our head in bemusement or confusion.

If you want to work with your dreams, you need to be able to understand them. This can be tricky because many, if not most, of our dreams are cloaked in imagery and symbols. As a result, interpretation is key. With the correct interpretation, even the strangest dreams can reveal their meanings. People often feel that a weird dream couldn't possibly be anything other than just a weird dream. However, a dream will usually make perfect sense and reveal its meanings to us once we have learned how to decode its messages, no matter how bizarre the dream may seem. This is something you can learn to do.

So let's turn our attention to learning how to interpret dreams. In order to do that, we'll need to start by learning some more basics about dreams.

Sources of Dreams

The first thing to know is that our dreams can stem from different sources. Even though most people feel that all dreams come from our unconscious, the truth is that there are indeed different possible sources that our dreams can spring from. These varied sources include the following.

Mental Processes

One of the functions of sleep and dreams is mental maintenance. While we're sleeping, a part of our mind and brain is performing maintenance for our mind, including sorting through the day's experiences, filing away memories, comparing memories and experiences to prior ones, and learning (consolidating what was learned during the day). This mental maintenance by itself will trigger dreams.

Your Unconscious

Your unconscious performs a lot of tasks for your mind and also contains your old personal stuff (fears, wishes, etc.). It doesn't stop working, so some of your dreams will stem from your unconscious while it's doing its work and expressing itself, as well as expressing and working on those fears and wants.

Other People or Beings

While you're sleeping, others can communicate with you. Passed-on loved ones who can't get through to us while we're awake will often whisper to us while we're sleeping. However, it's not just passed-on loved ones who can communicate with us. Living people we know, guides and other ethereal beings, and even our higher soul awareness can communicate with us while we're sleeping. These communications often take shape for us as dreams—dreams that may reflect the communication that took place.

Physical Conditions

Your physical condition will often color and affect your dream content. For example, if your bladder is full and you need to get to the bathroom, you may have what I call "bathroom dreams," in which you try to get to the bathroom but are prevented from doing so because the stalls are full or there's a long line. Additionally, some medications can affect sleep quality and dream content due to their effects on the body. Even what we had to drink or eat before bedtime can color our dreams. Another physical condition that can be a source of dreams is illness. There have been cases of a person dreaming that he or she had an illness, going for a check-up as a result, and learning that the illness was real. (This latter instance is an example of an intuitive or "psychic" dream, in which dream content may be telling us something we are consciously unaware of.)

External Conditions

External conditions can also affect dream content. For example, a loud noise or a cooler temperature than normal may intrude upon your dream and create content in it.

Actual Experiences

Although we tend to feel that in our dreams we are always dreaming "about" something, the truth is that some of our dreams can be actual experiences. While you're sleeping, your consciousness or even your astral body can be off exploring other places or time periods (yes, including past lives). You may have had dreams that felt real and felt more like real experiences than just dreaming about something. This is why. They may indeed have been real experiences.

As you can see, not all your dreams spring from your unconscious. Instead, there are a variety of sources that your dreams can spring from in addition to your unconscious.

Types of Dreams

Now that you've learned about the different sources that can give rise to your dreams, the next thing to learn is that there are different types of dreams. From working with dreams over the years, I have identified the following types of dreams:

- Sorting out the day's activities and filing away memories
- Expression of bodily conditions
- Actual experiencing and exploring

- Messages (from others, such as passed-on loved ones, friends, guides, etc.)
- Communication dreams (two-way "conversations" with others)
- Expressing or working out personal issues
- Expressing fears and desires
- Creative inspiration and problem-solving
- Intuitive or psychic (whether precognitive, clairvoyant, etc.)
- Combinations of types

Please note that last category. Any one dream can indeed be a combination of types. Never overlook your mind's ability to be creative and combine different types of dreams into one.

It is important to know that there are different types of dreams because we usually don't need to interpret every dream. As I noted earlier, not every dream is significant. If a dream was solely that of mental maintenance, for example, without incorporating any significant content, it may not have any earth-shattering meaning for us.

How do you begin to interpret your dreams?

Well, intuition is key. Dream dictionaries abound these days, and you may want to start by consulting them until you've developed and honed your intuition enough for better interpretation. You'll tend to be able to get only generic meanings from them, though.

For dreams stemming from our unconscious, we will all have our own vocabulary. A symbol in your dream may have a specific meaning only to you that you won't find in a dream dictionary. For example, years ago I had a dream in which there was a box of coins buried in the back yard. If I had consulted a dream dictionary for the meaning of coins, I might have found a meaning of wealth or value. However, in real life at that time my father had been collecting coins, so for me there was meaning connected to my father.

When interpreting dreams, it's imperative to find the valid meaning(s) for the dreamer—and any one dream can have more than one valid meaning for the person who had the dream. One trap that many people fall into is coming up with their own spin on someone else's dream. Again, it's crucial to find the meaning(s) that apply to the person who had the dream, not your meaning or a universal meaning.

We can determine this by dialoguing with the dreamer about what the symbols mean to him or her. For example, you can ask him or her, "What do you think of when you think of a (symbol)?" We can also use our intuition to know what the symbols in our dreams mean and what the total meaning(s) of the dream may be for the dreamer. This is why intuition is so important to interpreting dreams, sometimes even to intuitive and psychic dreams.

Before we go through the procedure to interpret dreams, I have some tips for you to keep in mind.

Tips for Interpreting Dreams
Pay Attention to How You Felt in the Dream and upon Awakening

Sometimes the emotion we felt in a dream can be a key to its meaning. When I spoke on dreams about six years ago, one attendee said that she had recurring dreams of being chased. Of course, the first thing you would think is that the dream was expressing a fear or anxiety. I asked her how she felt in her dreams, and she indicated that they were pleasant and that she enjoyed them. So, for her, being chased wasn't scary, and these were not scary dreams.

Pay Attention to Puns and Plays on Words

Your unconscious loves puns and plays on words! It also frequently expresses them in images and pictures. So allow yourself to be on the lookout for those puns and plays on words and the symbolic meanings they might have. For example, if you dream of cats, the dream may have to do with people you know named Katz. Or if you dream of trying to pick up a bucket and being unable to do so, the meaning may be that you can't get a handle on something.

Dreams Can Be Highly Symbolic or Literal

In your rush to tease out the meaning(s) of symbols, don't forget that some dreams or segments of dreams may be literal. For example, if you dream about being in a classroom, it could symbolically mean that you're learning some personal lessons in your life. However, it could also have a literal meaning of being in a classroom, especially if you're attending school or college when you have the dream.

Allow Yourself to Respect Your Dreams

I've heard people say over and over again, when telling me a dream, "It was so bizarre." The problem with seeing a dream as simply bizarre is that we'll then tend to discount it and feel that it couldn't possibly have any valuable meaning for us. When we have that attitude, it's a lot less likely that we'll be able to figure it out. So allow yourself to realize that, even if your dream seems totally strange and bizarre, it will probably have useful meanings for you, once you've been able to interpret it and grasp its meanings.

Use Your Intuition to Get the True Meaning(s) of Dreams

As I mentioned earlier, intuition is key in interpreting dreams, especially when you're interpreting someone else's dream. Please remember that you want to find the true meaning(s) for that person and not what the dream might mean for you. Using your intuition can help you do that.

You'll want to keep these things in mind as you work on interpreting dreams.

The next thing to do is to learn a step-by-step procedure for interpreting dreams. I created this procedure over the years through working with and interpreting many dreams. It will give you both a procedure and a blueprint for parsing out the meanings of dreams, so let's take a look at it. It includes both things to do and questions to ask.

Procedure for Interpreting Dreams

1. What type of dream is it? (Do you need to work with it? Is it significant?)

2. How did you feel in the dream and during different parts of the dream? How did you feel upon awakening?

3. Go over the dream in detail in a relaxed state of consciousness. What goes through your mind? (Use your intuition here.) It's important to note that you want to review the dream in as much detail as possible. If someone else is telling you his or her dream, a summary of the dream is not sufficient. Ask the person to relate the dream to you from beginning to end in detail.

4. Work with each symbol or element in the dream. Ask, "What does this mean to me (or to the person who had the dream)?"

5. Pay attention to any prominent words or phrases in the dream. Are there any puns or plays on words? If so, what are their meanings?

6. What is the general theme of the dream? What area of your life does it relate to?

7. Break the dream down into its story segments as if you're storyboarding it, especially if it's a longer dream. Then focus on understanding each discrete unit. (Use your intuition.)

8. Put all the segments together. What picture emerges? How does each segment relate to other segments? (Use your intuition.)

9. Look for any elements that may have particular significance for you due to your interests or activities. For example, if you're an astrologer, a bull in your dream could be signifying Taurus or the time frame of that sign.

10. Look at other people appearing in the dream. How do you feel about them? Consider that other people

in your dream could represent parts of yourself that you're not embracing, have disowned, or have suppressed.

11. What meaning(s) emerge from the dream? What is it telling you?

It may take you some time to assimilate this procedure and use it to your advantage, along with the other information and tips. However, it will all be worth the time and effort as you become increasingly able to derive the full meanings of dreams, both yours and others'.

You'll probably find over time that you're understanding your dreams more and more easily and are able to use them as a significant tool in your life for personal/spiritual unfolding, growth, insight, and problem-solving. Dreams give us many gifts. Enjoy your dreams and the process of unwrapping their gifts—and remember to use your intuition with them!

Recommended Reading

There are many excellent books on intuition, and reading them can give you even more insight into intuition and your own expression of it. The following are just a few that I recommend.

Brandon, Diane. *Invisible Blueprints: Intuitive Insights for Fulfillment in Life.* Sevierville, TN: Insight Publishing, 2005.

Hunt, Valerie V. *Infinite Mind: Science of the Human Vibrations of Consciousness.* Malibu, CA: Malibu Publishing, 1996.

Naparstek, Belleruth. *Your Sixth Sense: Activating Your Psychic Potential.* San Francisco, CA: HarperCollins, 1997.

Rosanoff, Nancy. *Intuition Workout: A Practical Guide to Discovering and Developing Your Inner Knowing.* Santa Rosa, CA: Aslan Publishing, 1991.

Bibliography

ABC-of-Yoga.com, "Meditation: Benefits of Meditation," accessed December 10, 2012, http://www.abc-of-yoga .com/meditation/benefits.asp.

About.com, "To Help You Sleep," updated June 21, 2006.

Allen, Colin. "The Benefits of Meditation." *Psychology Today*, April 1, 2003.

Altered States, "What Is the Function of the Various Brainwaves?," accessed December 10, 2012, http://altered-states.net/barry/newsletter217/index.htm.

BBC News, "Duke Nukem Sheds Light on Brain," April 18, 2006, accessed December 10, 2012, http://news.bbc.co .uk/2/hi/science/nature/4908484.stm.

———, "'Sleepless Grumps' Seen in Brain," October 23, 2007, accessed December 10, 2012, http://news.bbc.co.uk/2/hi/health/7056611.stm.

———, "Sweet Smells Foster Sweet Dreams," September 22, 2008, accessed December 10, 2012, http://news.bbc.co.uk/2/hi/health/7628744.stm.

Bradt, Steve, "Study Finds the Mind Is a Frequent, but Not Happy, Wanderer," Physorg.com, November 11, 2010, accessed December 10, 2012, http://phys.org/news/2010-11-mind-frequent-happy.html.

Brehm, Barbara A., EdD, "Exercise and Stress," *eFitness Direct,* 2001, accessed December 10, 2012, http://www.efitnessdirect.com/fitness_tips.php.

Cartwright, Rosalind D. *The Twenty-Four Hour Mind: The Role of Sleep and Dreaming in Our Emotional Lives.* New York: Oxford University Press, 2010.

Centers for Disease Control and Prevention, "CDC Study Reveals Adults May Not Get Enough Rest or Sleep," February 28, 2008, access December 10, 2012, http://www.cdc.gov/media/pressrel/2008/r080228.htm.

Chicago Press Release Services, "Can't Sleep? Maybe It's Your Computer," accessed December 10, 2012, http://chicagopressrelease.com/news/can%E2%80%99t-sleep-maybe-it%E2%80%99s-your-computer.

Childre, Doc Lew, *Freeze Frame: Fast-Action Stress Relief: A Scientifically Proven Technique,* Boulder Creek, CA: Planetary Publications, 1994.

Childre, Doc Lew, and Rollin McCraty. "Love: The Hidden Power of the Heart: A Scientific Perspective." *Caduceus Journal* 26 (1998).

China Daily, "Don't Think, Feel," April 2, 2008, accessed December 10, 2012, http://www.chinadaily.com.cn /citylife/2008-04/02/content_6585451.htm.

CNN.com, "Daydreaming Is Brain's Default Setting, Study Finds," January 19, 2007.

Cromie, William J., "Meditation Found to Increase Brain Size," *Harvard Gazette*, February 2, 2006, accessed December 10, 2012, http://news.harvard.edu/gazette /story/2006/02/meditation-found-to-increase-brain-size.

Crossroads Institute, "Brainwaves and EEG: The Language of the Brain," n.d., accessed June 7, 2005.

CTV News, "Cellphone Radiation May Ruin a Good Night's Sleep," January 21, 2008, accessed December 12, 2012, http://www.ctvnews.ca/cellphone-radiation-may-ruin-a -good-night-s-sleep-1.272194.

Daily Times, "Lack of Deep Sleep Raise [*sic*] Diabetes Risk," January 7, 2008, accessed December 10, 2012, http:// www.dailytimes.com.pk/default.asp?page=2008\01\07 \story_7-1-2008_pg6_14.

Davis, Angela, "Stress Can Degrade Your Health in Surprising Ways," WCCO, January 21, 2008.

Davis, Eric W., "Gifted Chinese Children Teleport Objects without Damage," Sympathetic Vibratory Physics, February 7, 2008, accessed December 10, 2012, http://www.svpvril .com/svpnotes/T/TELEPORTATION,_195535.html.

Doheny, Kathleen, "TV Could Be Disrupting Your Kid's Sleep," *U. S. News & World Report*, February 25, 2008, accessed December 10, 2012, http://health.usnews.com /usnews/health/healthday/080225/tv-could-be -disrupting-your-kids-sleep.htm.

Dworak, Marianna, "Meditation Does a Brain Good," *The Daily Free Press*, September 16, 2008.

Foster, Russell, "Bring Back the Night—Your Health and Wellbeing Depend on it," *The Guardian*, July 13, 2011, accessed December 10, 2012, http://www.guardian.co .uk/science/2011/jul/13/neuroscience-biology.

Fountain, Henry, "Study Gives Key Role to Sleep in Helping Brain Learn Anew," *The New York Times*, January 29, 2008, accessed December 10, 2012, http://www.nytimes .com/2008/01/29/science/29obslee.html.

Gladwell, Malcolm. *Blink: The Power of Thinking Without Thinking*. New York: Little, Brown and Company, 2005.

Guthrie, Catherine, "The Light-Cancer Connection," *Prevention*, December 15, 2005, accessed December 10, 2012, http://www.prevention.com/health/health -concerns/kick-these-cancer-related-habits?page=2.

Haederle, Michael, "Getting a Handle on Why We Sleep," *Pacific Standard*, November 25, 2008, accessed December 10, 2012, http://www.psmag.com/health /getting-a-handle-on-why-we-sleep-4097.

Hardt, James V., PhD, "Alpha Waves—Alpha Brain Waves," Biocybernaut Institute.

———,"Alpha Brain Waves and Biofeedback Science," Biocybernaut Institute, accessed August 30, 2003.

Helpguide.org, "Understanding Stress: Signs, Symptoms, Causes, and Effects," accessed December 10, 2012, http://www.helpguide.org/mental/stress_signs.htm.

Hirschler, Ben, "Lack of Sleep May be Deadly, Research Shows," *Reuters*, September 24, 2007, accessed December 10, 2012, http://www.reuters.com/article/2007/09/24/us -sleep-death-idUSL2462796020070924.

Houston, Jean. *The Possible Human: A Course in Enhancing Your Physical, Mental, and Creative Abilities.* New York: Jeremy P. Tarcher/Putnam, 1982.

Hunt, Valerie V. *Infinite Mind: Science of the Human Vibrations of Consciousness.* Malibu, CA: Malibu Publishing, 1996.

Institute of HeartMath, "Coincidence or Intuition?," reprinted by Macquarie Institute, accessed December 10, 2012, http://www.macquarieinstitute.com/company /proom/pr/intuition_study.html.

———. *Freeze-Frame Training Guidebook.* Boulder Creek, CA: Institute of HeartMath, 1996. Handout given during lecture by Joseph Sundram at Conference of Institute of Noetic Sciences, 1996.

———, "The Freeze-Frame Technique May Be Beneficial in the Control of Hypertension," n.d., accessed April 20, 2002.

———, "Heart Rate Variability Tachograms: Hour-Long Examples," n.d., accessed April 20, 2002.

———. *IHM ResearchUpdate* 2, no. 1 (1995).

————, "Worry and Anxiety Can Cause Hormonal Imbalances and Age You Faster: New Research Explains Why and Offers Solutions," July 17, 1996.

KansasCity.com, "To Sleep, Perchance to Remember," January 3, 2007.

Kaufman, Marc, "Meditation Gives Brain a Charge, Study Finds," *Washington Post,* January 3, 2005, accessed December 10, 2012, http://www.washingtonpost.com /wp-dyn/articles/A43006-2005Jan2.html.

Lemon, Sarah, "Learning to Sleep: Insomnia Carries Many Risks, Including Troubling Health Consequences," *Mail Tribune,* May 06, 2008, accessed December 10, 2012, http://www.mailtribune.com/apps/pbcs.dll /article?AID=/20080506/LIFE/805060307.

Licauco, Jaime, "Are You a Right- or Left-Brain Thinker?" *Philippine Daily Inquirer,* July 4, 2006, accessed December 10, 2012, http://showbizandstyle.inquirer.net/lifestyle /lifestyle/view/20060704-7961/Are_you_a_right-_or_left -brain_thinker%3F.

Life Science Foundation, "Oxytocin: World's Expert Talks about This Calming Hormone," accessed December 10, 2012, http://lifesciencefoundation.org/cmoxtyocin.html.

Maes, Nancy, "Music as Medicine: Therapy Is Clinically Valid for the Living and the Dying," *Chicago Tribune,* March 9, 2008.

Martin, Howard, "Activating the Heart's Intelligence," Institute of HeartMath, n.d.

Mayo Clinic, "Stress Symptoms: Effects on Your Body, Feelings, and Behavior," February 20, 2007, accessed

December 10, 2012, http://www.mayoclinic.com/health/stress-symptoms/SR00008_D.

McAuliffe, Kathleen, "Stomach Problems: The Truth Behind Your Gut Feelings," *More Magazine,* February 2005, accessed online December 10, 2012, http://www.more.com/health/wellness/stomach-problems-truth-behind-your-gut-feelings?.

McCraty, Rollin, MA, Mike Atkinson, William A. Tiller, PhD, Glen Rein, PhD, and Alan D. Watkins, MBBS, "The Effects of Emotions on Short-Term Power Spectrum Analysis of Heart Rate Variability," *The American Journal of Cardiology* 76, no. 14 (November 15, 1995): 1089–93.

McCraty, Rollin, and Doc Childre, "The Grateful Heart: The Psychophysiology of Appreciation," in *The Psychology of Gratitude*, edited by R. A. Emmons and M. E. McCullough (New York: Oxford University Press, 2004), 230–55.

McGregor, Jena, "Why Sleep Deprivation Can Make You Unethical," *Washington Post,* May 13, 2011, accessed December 10, 2012, http://www.washingtonpost.com/blogs/post-leadership/post/why-sleep-deprivation-canmakeyou-unethical/2011/04/01/AFIIxT2G_blog.html.

MedHeadlines, "Chronic Sleep Disruption Leads to Heart, Kidney Disease," March 19, 2008, accessed December 10, 2012, http://medheadlines.com/2008/03/chronic-sleep-disruption-leads-to-heart-kidney-disease.

Medical News Today, "Light at Night Is Dangerous to Health," January 29, 2007, accessed December 10, 2102, http://www.medicalnewstoday.com/releases/61808.php.

Michigan State University, "Sleep Helps Reduce Errors in Memory, Research Suggests," September 10, 2009, accessed December 10, 2012, http://msutoday.msu.edu /news/2009/sleep-helps-reduce-errors-in-memory-msu -research-suggests.

Naparstek, Belleruth. *Your Sixth Sense: Activating Your Psychic Potential.* San Francisco, CA: HarperCollins, 1997.

Ojile, Dr. Joseph, "Studying Sleep for Our Better Health, Wellness," *St. Louis Post-Dispatch,* September 10, 2008.

Olson, Geoff, "Not Getting Enough Sleep? It Could Be Hazardous to Your Health," *Common Ground,* May 2008, accessed December 10, 2012, http://www.common ground.ca/iss/202/cg202_sleep.shtml.

Rafill, Thomas E. "China's Super Psychics Revisited: Older Children Are Learning Super Psychic Abilities," *Spirit of Ma'at* 1 (October 2000), accessed December 10, 2012, http://www.spiritofmaat.com/archive/oct1/prns/pdong .htm.

Rajapakse, Nimal, PhD, "The Science of Meditation," *Daily News,* May 9, 2007, accessed December 10, 2012, http:// www.dailynews.lk/2007/05/09/fea05.asp.

Ramachandran, V. S., MD, PhD. *A Brief Tour of Human Consciousness: From Impostor Poodles to Purple Numbers.* New York: Pi Press, 2004.

Ramachandran, V. S., MD, PhD, and Sandra Blakeslee. *Phantoms in the Brain: Probing the Mysteries of the Human Mind.* New York: William Morrow, 1998.

Real Simple, "Tips to Get the Sleep You Crave," reprinted by CNN.com, March 4, 2008, accessed December 10, 2012, http://www.cnn.com/2008/LIVING/personal/03/04/good.sleep/index.html.

Ring, Kenneth. *Heading Toward Omega: In Search of the Meaning of the Near-Death Experience.* New York: William Morrow, 1984.

Roan, Shari, "Cheating Sleep Can Prove Costly," *Los Angeles Times,* March 31, 2008.

Robertson, Duncan, "Sleeping Less Than Six Hours a Night 'Doubles Risk of Heart Disease,'" *Daily Mail,* May 2, 2008.

Rock, Andrea. *The Mind at Night.* New York: Basic Books, 2004.

Rojas-Burke, Joe, "Scientists Study Links between Brain, Meditation," *The Oregonian,* June 19, 2008, accessed December 10, 2012, http://www.oregonlive.com/health/index.ssf/2008/06/scientists_study_links_between.html.

Rosanoff, Nancy. *Intuition Workout: A Practical Guide to Discovering and Developing Your Inner Knowing.* Santa Rosa, CA: Aslan Publishing, 1991.

Rubin, Rita, "Babies Gain Weight with Less Sleep," *USA Today,* April 7, 2008, accessed December 10, 2012, http://usatoday30.usatoday.com/news/health/2008-04-07-sleep-weight_N.htm.

Science Daily, "Loss of Sleep, Even for a Single Night, Increases Inflammation in the Body," September 4, 2008, accessed December 10, 2012, http://www.sciencedaily.com/releases/2008/09/080902075211.htm.

Smith, Rebecca, "Meditation 'Cuts Risk of Heart Attack by Half,'" *The Telegraph*, November 17, 2009, accessed December 10, 2012, http://www.telegraph.co.uk/health/healthnews/6581495/Meditation-cuts-risk-of-heart-attack-by-half.html.

Tierney, John, "Discovering the Virtues of a Wandering Mind," *The New York Times*, June 28, 2010, accessed December 10, 2012, http://www.nytimes.com/2010/06/29/science/29tier.html.

The Times of India, "Prolonged Lack of Sleep Affects Brain," May 21, 2008, reprinted at Find Me a Cure, accessed December 10, 2012, http://findmeacure.com/2008/05/22/prolonged-lack-of-sleep-affects-brain.

The University of Chicago Medicine, "Sleep Loss Boosts Appetite, May Encourage Weight Gain," December 6, 2004, accessed December 10, 2012, http://www.uchospitals.edu/news/2004/20041206-sleep.html.

USA Today, "Sleep Essential for Creative Thinking, Study Says," January 21, 2004, accessed December 10, 2012, http://usatoday30.usatoday.com/news/health/2004-01-21-sleep-creativity_x.htm.

*Web*MD, "Stress Can Affect You Both Immediately (Acute Stress) and Over Time (Chronic Stress)," April 25, 2007.

Weil, Dr. Andrew, "Aromatherapy Shows Promising Results for Sleep," *The Calgary Herald*, March 31, 2008, accessed December 10, 2012, http://www.canada.com/calgaryherald/news/reallife/story.html?id=8bb08f51-49c9-421c-8fdf-795c99cc7f70.

———, "Trouble Sleeping? Try Jasmine," *Dr. Andrew Weil's Daily Health Tips*, December 17, 2010, accessed December 10, 2012, http://www.drweilblog.com/home/2010/12/17/trouble-sleeping-try-jasmine.html.

Wenger, Win, PhD, and Richard Poe. *The Einstein Factor: A Proven New Method for Increasing Your Intelligence.* Westminster, MD: Prima Publishing, 1996.

Wiley, T. S., with Bent Formby. *Lights Out: Sleep, Sugar, and Survival.* New York: Pocket Books, 2000.

Wise, Anna, *The High-Performance Mind: Mastering Brainwaves for Insight, Healing, and Creativity,* New York: G. P. Putnam's Sons, 1995.

To Write to the Author

If you wish to contact the author or would like more information about this book, please write to the author in care of Llewellyn Worldwide Ltd., and we will forward your request. Both the author and publisher appreciate hearing from you and learning of your enjoyment of this book and how it has helped you. Llewellyn Worldwide Ltd. cannot guarantee that every letter written to the author can be answered, but all will be forwarded. Please write to:

Diane Brandon
℅ Llewellyn Worldwide
2143 Wooddale Drive
Woodbury, MN 55125-2989

Please enclose a self-addressed stamped envelope for reply,
or $1.00 to cover costs. If outside the USA, enclose
an international postal reply coupon.

GET MORE AT LLEWELLYN.COM

Visit us online to browse hundreds of our books and decks, plus sign up to receive our e-newsletters and exclusive online offers.

- **Free tarot readings • Spell-a-Day • Moon phases**
- **Recipes, spells, and tips • Blogs • Encyclopedia**
- **Author interviews, articles, and upcoming events**

GET SOCIAL WITH LLEWELLYN

Find us on  🐦 **@LlewellynBooks**

www.Facebook.com/LlewellynBooks

GET BOOKS AT LLEWELLYN

LLEWELLYN ORDERING INFORMATION

Order online: Visit our website at www.llewellyn.com to select your books and place an order on our secure server.

Order by phone:
- Call toll free within the US at 1-877-NEW-WRLD (1-877-639-9753)
- We accept VISA, MasterCard, American Express, and Discover.
- Canadian customers must use credit cards.

Order by mail:
Send the full price of your order (MN residents add 6.875% sales tax) in US funds plus postage and handling to: Llewellyn Worldwide, 2143 Wooddale Drive, Woodbury, MN 55125-2989

POSTAGE AND HANDLING

STANDARD (US):
(Please allow 12 business days)
$30.00 and under, add $6.00.
$30.01 and over, FREE SHIPPING.

INTERNATIONAL ORDERS,
INCLUDING CANADA:
$16.00 for one book, plus $3.00 for each additional book.

Visit us online for more shipping options. Prices subject to change.

FREE CATALOG!

To order, call
1-877-
NEW-WRLD
ext. 8236
or visit our
website

KATHRYN HARWIG

The

RETURN

of

INTUITION

Awakening Psychic Gifts
in the Second Half of Life

The Return of Intuition
Awakening Psychic Gifts in the Second Half of Life
KATHRYN HARWIG

Natural psychic sensitivity is often associated with children. However, *The Return of Intuition* reveals a little-known, widespread phenomenon of profound intuitive awakening occurring in adults—usually around the age of fifty.

Bringing this remarkable trend to light is psychic medium Kathryn Harwig, who has helped clients nationwide understand, nurture, and embrace their newfound psychic awareness. Their inspiring stories highlight what triggers this life-changing gift—usually illness or the death of a loved one—and how it can be used to aid others, receive messages from friends and family in spirit, and begin life anew with confidence, courage, and clarity. Affirming the joys of aging, this unique spiritual guide offers comfort and support to the elders of our society, encouraging them to reclaim their once-revered roles—as the crone, shaman, and sage—by passing on spiritual wisdom to a new generation.

978-0-7387-1880-4, 216 pp., 5 ³/₁₆ x 8   **$15.95**

LOVE
and
INTUITION

A Psychic's Guide
to Creating Lasting Love

SHERRIE DILLARD

Love and Intuition

A Psychic's Guide to Creating Lasting Love
SHERRIE DILLARD

Love, by its very nature, is profoundly spiritual. Each of us can harness this transformative emotion by embracing our own natural intuition.

Building on the success of *Discover Your Psychic Type*, professional psychic Sherrie Dillard presents a life-changing paradigm based on the four love types. This unique book teaches you to develop your intuition to attract and sustain love, while enriching your relationship with your spouse or partner, friends, and yourself.

Once you find out your intuitive love type—emotional, spiritual, mental, or physical—you can then determine your spouse or partner's love type, and learn practical ways to strengthen your relationship and heighten intimacy.

978-0-7387-1555-1, 336 pp., 6 x 9   **$16.95**

DISCOVER YOUR
Inner Wisdom
THROUGH
Dowsing

Intuition
in an
Instant

KATHRYN KLVANA

Intuition in an Instant
Discover Your Inner Wisdom Through Dowsing
Kathyrn Klvana

Kick-start your intuition with a practical, easy-to-learn skill that will have countless uses in your life. Learn how age-old techniques for finding water can help you get an answer to any question instantly, giving you intuitive guidance on the spot whenever you need it.

Most people prefer to use a small pendulum when asking intuitive questions, rather than the classic forked stick or Y-rod. You'll learn to trust your intuition and make better decisions, remove blocks that are keeping you from achieving your dreams, and become more effective at work. You can use the knowledge gained from dowsing to improve your relationships, enhance your health, even communicate with your pets. Save time, energy, and money by using this simple form of divination.

978-0-7387-2330-3, 240 pp., 5 x 7   **$14.95**

Ignite Your Psychic Intuition

An
A to Z Guide
to Developing Your
Sixth Sense

Teresa Brady

Ignite Your Psychic Intuition
An A to Z Guide to Developing Your Sixth Sense
Teresa Brady

Developing your psychic powers doesn't have to take a lot of time and patience. *Ignite Your Psychic Intuition* proves that we can easily tap into our sixth sense, even with the busiest of lifestyles.

In this innovative and easy-to-use guide, Teresa Brady demystifies psychic and intuitive development and step-by-step shows you how to unlock and heighten your extrasensory perception. Designed in an A-to-Z format, this book offers twenty-six practical teaching tools, one for each letter of the alphabet. Discover the four main types of intuitive communication—clairvoyance, clairaudience, clairsentience, and claircognizance—and how to use them to enhance your life.

Beginners and experienced practitioners looking for new ideas will enjoy developing their higher senses through white light bathing, energy scans, salt showers, directed dreaming, chakra cleansing, and crystal gazing.

978-0-7387-2170-5, 288 pp., 5 x 7 **$15.99**